Douglas Rodriguez is one of the most innovative chefs in America today. He concocts dishes from extraordinary combinations of ingredients which result in some of the most complex, tantalizing food around. While this food transports me to the sunny tropic where exotic fruits, sugar cane, chiles, and succulent seafood are typical fare, there is nothing terribly typical about this marvelous Nuevo Latino food.

—Stephan Pyles, Star Canyon

The cuisine, the recipes, and the culinary style of Douglas Rodriguez are as exciting as they are refreshing. This book shows very well his passion for Latin foods and his "Nuevo Latino." What a wonderful idea for a book.

—Larry Forgione, An American Place

Douglas is one of those people who epitomize the grander aspects of the world, like Thomas Wolfe, Babe Ruth, or Caruso. His immense talent, his joy, his uncensored curiosity well out of him and you become undeniably warmed and gladdened by them, by him. He is one of the "awakeners" to the emerging flavors, traditional as well as newly created, of Nuevo Latino and New World cuisines.

—Norman Van Aken, Norman's

A meal with Douglas Rodriguez is a thrill! A forkful of his robust Ensalada Bacalao; a plate of tangy Swordfish Escabeche with those addictive, crunchy tostones, the lingering savor of Plantain-crusted Mahimahi with that sweet-savory tropical mash called fufu (of which I never seem to get enough)—it all tastes of heritage and tradition, yet it's as up-to the minute as Fifth Avenue. I hope *Nuevo Latino* opens a world of eyes (and taste buds) to the beautiful richness of Latin flavor.

—Rick Bayless, Frontera Grill

NUEVO LATINO

Recipes that Celebrate the New Latin American Cuisine

Douglas Rodriguez

WITH

John Harrisson

PHOTOGRAPHY BY

Dennis Galante

TEN SPEED PRESS
Berkeley / Toronto

A portion of the proceeds from the sale of each book will be donated to The James Beard Foundation, an institution dedicated to promoting culinary excellence.

Photography © 2002, 1995 by Dennis Galante

Cover and text design by Nancy Austin

Map on page vi by Wendy Wallin Mallinow

People art throughout by Jose Ortega

Photo on page ii: Hearts of Palm and Orange Salad with Mâche

🔟 TEN SPEED PRESS
P.O. Box 7123
Berkeley, California 94707

Library of Congress Cataloging-in-Publication Data
Rodriguez, Douglas.
  Nuevo latino : recipes that celebrate the new Latin-American cuisine / Douglas Rodriguez with John Harrison ; photography by Dennis Galante.
      p. cm.
Includes bibliographical references and index.
  ISBN 1-58008-380-3 (pbk.)
  I. Cookery, Latin American. I. Harrison, John.
II. Title.
  TX716 .R63 2002
  641.598—dc21

                                    2002000500

Printed in China

1 2 3 4 5 6 7 8 9 10 — 06 05 04 03 02

CONTENTS

ACKNOWLEDGMENTS

SPECIAL THANKS are due to a number of individuals and compadres who have made this book possible:

First, of course, to my mom, my dad, and my brother Frank.

Bernie Matz and Carlos Prio, my first business partners at The Wet Paint Cafe in Miami Beach—thanks for giving me my first break.

Liz Balmaseda, for my first food write-up in the *Tropic Magazine* section of *The Miami Herald*—true motivation for a starving artist.

Efrain Veiga and the late Elly Levy, my partners at Yuca. I am eternally grateful for your believing in me.

Phil Suarez and Bob Giraldi, my current partners and friends, who brought me to New York so that I could spread the word.

All my sous chefs, and especially Bernie Matz, Andrew DiCataldo, Guillermo Veloso, and Alex Garcia.

Frank Thorn, for giving me my first kitchen experiences; Felipe Rojas Lombardi—you were a true inspiration; Raymond Sokolov, whose book helped inspire my career; and my Miami colleagues in The Mango Gang.

Dennis Galante, my photographer, for the wonderful images of food; John Harrisson, my agent and editor, for organizing and fine-tuning the text; and Phil Wood, Kirsty Melville, and all my friends at Ten Speed Press for making this book a reality.

A very special thank you to Keith Stupell, who gave us unlimited access to his collection of beautiful and exotic plates for the food photography.

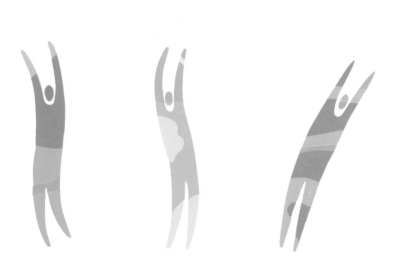

INTRODUCTION

IF I HAD WRITTEN THIS BOOK four or five years ago, it might have been called *Nuevo Cubano* because I'm a first-generation Cuban-American and the food I was cooking in Miami was based on the Cuban food that I grew up with. A few years ago, however, I became fascinated by the melting pot of Latin flavors and cuisines that Miami offered. After tasting new combinations of familiar ingredients and exciting dishes from South America and the Caribbean, I began traveling and making new friends from these areas. I decided I wanted to explore these Latin traditions and translate them into my own style, introducing them into the North American mainstream. This was the foundation for my cuisine— Nuevo Latino.

To me, food is a passion. My hobby is eating at new places, tasting new foods, and trying different ethnic cuisines—I can't think of one cuisine I don't like. I enjoy putting together different textures and contrasts of flavors, colors, and heat intensities. I strongly believe that people eat not only to assuage their hunger but also to feel better, and that motivates me to create and cook dishes that make people feel *great.* My passion for food started very early. I grew up on the Upper West Side of Manhattan, where my parents met after having left Cuba in 1955, before the revolution. I remember that even as a kid I liked to hang around the kitchen and watch my mother—a naturally gifted cook—prepare the traditional foods of her homeland. I'd help, too, when she'd let me. Even then I was fascinated by the process of mixing ingredients to make delicious things to eat. My mother taught me all the basics, even if most of the time she was trying to push me outside to play.

The traveling my family did when I was growing up exposed me to many different cuisines early in life. We vacationed in Venezuela, Mexico, and Costa Rica as well as in Spain, Belgium, Italy, and Germany. In Spain, at age ten, I ordered a tortilla—an omelet with potatoes and onions— and asked for tomato ketchup. When the waiter brought some tomato paste mixed with water I thought I was going to die. No way could I manage without real ketchup! These early experiences were stimulation for my mind and palate.

By the time I was thirteen, my hobby was buying cookbooks at garage sales, and it was around that time that I bought my own set of pots and pans. I spent a lot of time creating recipes in the kitchen, and to this day my family has humorous tales to tell of some of these early "experiments."

When I was fourteen, we moved from New York to Miami, and I landed my first serious kitchen job. As an apprentice for the summer at the Four Ambassadors Hotel, I was rotated through several kitchen positions. The experience of working at different positions was invaluable, and cooking just seemed to come naturally to me. Besides, working with a knife and creating dishes brought out my artistic side and that was very exciting for me.

By seventeen I had memorized much of Escoffier and other classics. On weekends, I worked part time in a Chinese restaurant, and when I left school, my first full-time job was as a breakfast cook at the prestigious Fountainebleau Hilton Hotel in Miami Beach. The busier it got, the more I liked it. It was at the Fountainebleau that I realized that this really was the life for me.

I went on to train in classic techniques and kitchen skills at Johnson and Wales University in Providence, and then returned to Miami, where I accepted a position as saucier at the Sonesta Beach Hotel. But my real break came when I was approached by Bernie Matz and Carlos Prio, who were planning to open The Wet Paint Cafe in Miami Beach within a few weeks, and they asked me to join them as head chef and partner. I jumped at the opportunity.

At The Wet Paint Cafe, I had full control of the menu and so began my Nuevo Latino style of cooking. I continuously experimented with Latin ingredients in nontraditional ways. It was also where I developed a signature dish, Guava-Glazed Barbecued Ribs (page 128), which now appears on many menus and in several cookbooks. In 1989, I moved to Yuca, an upscale, Cuban-style restaurant in Coral Gables, Florida. After my first year there, I became a partner, and during the next three years I continued to apply new ideas and contemporary spins to traditional Latin dishes. I developed a passion for talking with the staff about their native foods and finding out whether a Cuban dish, for example, had a close counterpart in their homeland, or how ceviches were made where they were from. These lively conversations gave way to new ideas constantly.

While I was at Yuca, my creativity was undoubtedly spurred by the food revolution and renaissance that Miami was undergoing. During that period, I joined my talented colleagues (Norman Van Aken, Allen Susser, and Mark Militello) in The Mango Gang, as we were nicknamed, in cooking our variations of New World cuisine. It was this environment that inspired all of us to sample and develop new approaches—including trying Latin-based themes and foods—and to work toward new culinary heights.

It was, however, always in the back of my mind that New York was the ultimate stage. When Phil Suarez and Bob Giraldi, who wanted to bring innovative Latin cuisine to New York, offered me a partnership at Patria, I relished the opportunity to introduce this exuberant style of cooking to the culinary capital of the world.

Before we opened Patria, on St. Valentine's Day in 1994, I traveled once more to the Caribbean and South America. What really surprised me was that the most outstanding food I tasted was in people's homes, not in restaurants. I brought back a wealth of experience and knowledge that I've been drawing on ever since, as I opened three other restaurants—Chicama and Pipa in Manhattan, and Alma de Cuba in Philadelphia.

I have been eating and cooking with Latin ingredients—beans, rice, tubers, and salsas—my entire life. These ingredients are the basics in most South and Central American countries, and even though they are considered the common man's foods, I have endeavored to bring new meaning to them, and the age-old dishes they comprise, through my cuisine. Nuevo Latino cuisine is a simple style of cooking, as the recipes in this book prove. I insist on using the freshest of ingredients and I bid you to do so as well.

Nuevo Latino means "new Latin." Here I have compiled a collection of dishes that incorporate multiple recipes. Therefore, you can enjoy the experience of *Nuevo Latino* cuisine simply by choosing a single dish and preparing the recipes that accompany it. It is with this novel approach to whole meals that use old, rediscovered ingredients that I have developed Nuevo Latino style.

Many Latins will recognize the foods from their homeland, but will notice that they are served in nontraditional ways. For many non-Latins, this book will be an adventure into the unknown and an introduction to dishes that instantly become new favorites. For me, cooking is all-consuming and a creative connection with my heritage. All of my dishes are founded on tradition and home cooking—the type of food I was raised on and still love. I invite you to enter my world of cooking…Nuevo Latino–style.

Buen provecho,

Douglas Rodriguez

NUEVO LATINO

TECHNIQUES &
BASIC RECIPES

Opposite page: key Nuevo Latino ingredients (left to right)—chayote, malanga (sometimes called taro), corn, boniato, yuca, cachucha peppers, sugarcane, and blue potatoes

THIS CHAPTER contains some essential "how-to" information for preparing ingredients that are used throughout the book. You'll also find basic recipes for stocks, pantry items, condiments, and adobos (marinades), which are the foundations of Nuevo Latino cuisine.

ELEMENTARY TECHNIQUES

ROASTING BELL PEPPERS AND CHILES

This cooking technique results in tender peppers or chiles with an intensely smoky flavor and enables you to remove the tough, bitter skins.

Prepare the grill, preferably using wood chips that have been soaked in water. Leaving the stems on, lightly brush the peppers or chiles with olive oil. Place on the hot grill, or pierce with a fork and hold over the open flame (even a stove-top gas burner can be used). Let the flame char the skins, rotating until they're evenly blackened.

Transfer the peppers or chiles to a large paper or plastic bag and seal the top. Let the peppers or chiles steam for 10 to 12 minutes, or until cooled. Remove them from the bag and peel off their skins. Cut off the stems, then remove and discard the seeds.

You can prepare roasted peppers and chiles ahead of time and store them by covering them with vegetable oil mixed with a small amount of finely minced garlic, if desired. Reserve in the refrigerator for up to 2 months.

TOASTING DRIED CHILES

Dried chiles should be toasted to bring out their full flavors. Preheat the oven to 250°. Seed the chiles with the tip of a knife and place them on a baking sheet. Toast in the oven for 15 to 20 minutes, then remove from the oven and let cool. Grind to a powder in a blender or rehydrate

in hot water for 20 minutes. The chile powder may be stored in an airtight container for 6 months.

ROASTING GARLIC

I like to use roasted garlic for its subtle, mellow, and slightly sweet garlicky flavor. Preheat the oven to 450°. Coat 3 heads of garlic with 1 tablespoon of olive oil and season with salt and pepper. Wrap the garlic in aluminum foil and place on a baking sheet. Roast in the oven for 20 to 25 minutes, or until soft. Remove from the oven and let cool. Squeeze out the roasted garlic from the cloves.

ROASTING TOMATOES, CORN, AND ONIONS

The roasting process gives tomatoes a smoky, charred flavor and brings out their sweet tones. Place the tomatoes on a prepared grill with wood chips (see the instructions for roasting chiles, but do not brush tomatoes with oil), on a rack set over a stove-top gas flame, or roast them individually by piercing each tomato with a fork and holding it over a gas flame. In each case, turn and roast the tomatoes until the skins are evenly blackened. Let cool, cut in half, and remove and discard the seeds. Use the rest of the tomato, including the blackened skin. (If you like, you can remove some of the skin for a less pronounced roasted flavor.) Roasted tomatoes may be stored covered in the refrigerator for up to 2 days. Corn and onion can also be roasted over the open flame. Brush cobs and onion halves with olive oil and roast until evenly blackened.

PEELING PLANTAINS

Green plantains are difficult to peel. Here's an easy way to do it: Fill your sink with very warm water. Cut off both ends of each plantain and make three or four slits lengthwise through the skin. Let the plantains sit in the water for about 10 minutes. Once they have soaked, you'll find that they can be easily peeled by running your fingers under the skin.

PEELING YUCA

Hold the yuca in your hand. With a heavy-duty large knife, make slashing motions down the length of the tuber, as if you were whittling but on a larger scale. Using a traditional vegetable peeler will not work because the skin is not only thick but is usually waxed to preserve the tuber while shipping.

TOASTING COCONUT

Preheat the oven to 350°. Spread store-bought unsweet-ened shredded coconut on an ungreased baking sheet. Toast in the oven for about 20 minutes, stirring frequently so that it becomes lightly browned all over.

TOASTING CUMIN

Toasted cumin has a fuller, deeper flavor than raw cumin. Heat a dry sauté pan or skillet and toast the cumin seeds over high heat for 3 to 4 minutes, or until they turn brown and become fragrant. Stir or shake the pan continuously so that the seeds brown evenly and do not burn.

ROASTING BONES FOR A DARKER STOCK

Chop the bones into a manageable size and transfer them to a heavy-bottomed stockpot. Add 3 tablespoons Annatto Oil (page 8). Cook and stir over medium-high heat for 10 minutes, then add the vegetables the recipe calls for and cook 5 more minutes. Continue as the stock recipe directs, adding all remaining ingredients to the stockpot.

GENERAL GUIDELINES

Here are some points of clarification about the ingredients used in the recipes:

- Always use fresh herbs instead of dried, unless otherwise stated. Discard the stems and use only the leaves, unless otherwise stated.

- Always use fresh ginger and garlic, unless otherwise stated.

- Onions, garlic, carrots, and gingerroot should always be peeled. However, when whole heads of garlic are called for in stocks, for example, remove any loose, papery covering but do not peel them.

- Use only sweet, unsalted butter, because the amount of sodium can be too variable in salted butter.

- Use either extra virgin (from the first pressing) or virgin (pure) olive oil, unless otherwise stated.

- Sugar refers to granulated, or white, sugar, unless otherwise stated.

- Whenever possible, use kosher salt, which has a better texture and flavor than table salt and is also additive-free.

- Unless otherwise stated, pepper refers to black pepper and should always be freshly ground.

- If at all possible, use only freshly squeezed citrus juice.

- All bell peppers and chiles should be stemmed, except when roasting them.

- When preparing the recipes that call for eggs "at room temperature," whether or not the eggs are to be cooked, use only the highest quality, salmonella-free eggs. For information about their availability see "Sources," (page 164). Use large-sized eggs when eggs are called for.

- Flour refers to all-purpose flour, unless otherwise stated.

PANTRY BASICS

Annatto Oil

Annatto seeds are used throughout South America for giving an attractive golden yellow color to rice and meat dishes. They are readily available in Latin markets.

1 cup vegetable or grapeseed oil
$^1/_2$ cup annatto seeds

In a saucepan, heat the oil and seeds together over low heat until the oil just begins to bubble, 8 to 10 minutes. Remove the pan from the heat and let the oil sit to become infused, about 3 hours.

Pour the oil slowly into a glass container, and discard the sediment. Cover the oil tightly. It will last up to 6 months stored in the refrigerator.

YIELD: APPROXIMATELY 1$^1/_2$ CUPS

Seasoned Flour

This is a hot and spicy seasoning to have on hand to coat chicken or fish for frying. However, if you do not want so much spice, you can adjust the amount of cayenne as desired.

1 pound all-purpose flour
2 tablespoons ground cayenne pepper
6 tablespoons paprika
3 tablespoons pepper
1 tablespoon ground cumin
3 tablespoons onion powder
3 tablespoons garlic powder
1 tablespoon ground allspice
1 tablespoon ground dried thyme

Sift all the ingredients together into a large mixing bowl, and store in an airtight container.

YIELD: APPROXIMATELY 3$^1/_4$ CUPS

Pickled Garlic

This useful condiment has a long shelf life, and doesn't have to be refrigerated. For best results, store in an airtight jar sealed with a rubber gasket. It can be used in salsas or on its own to complement grilled fish and it makes an interesting addition to crudité plates.

3 cups white wine vinegar
3 tablespoons sugar
3 tablespoons salt
8 heads garlic, broken up and peeled
3 sprigs thyme
8 peppercorns
2 bay leaves
1 tablespoon mustard seeds

In a saucepan, bring the vinegar, sugar, and salt to a boil and stir until the sugar and salt dissolve.

Place the garlic cloves in a glass storage jar and add the thyme, peppercorns, bay leaves, and mustard seeds. Pour the vinegar into the jar and let cool. Cover and store until needed.

YIELD: APPROXIMATELY 1 QUART

Perfect White Rice

Rice is a staple of Latin cuisines, and growing up in a Cuban family, I probably took it for granted. It was only when I left home that I realized how important well-cooked rice can be, both for the soul and other foods on the plate! I always try to impress on people that it's a sin to use converted or instant rice. It's got to be "real" rice, and preferably long-grain. Avoid flavoring rice, for that will detract from the flavors of the foods you're serving the rice with.

2 cups long-grain rice
2$^1/_2$ tablespoons vegetable oil
2 teaspoons salt
1 quart water

Rinse the rice in a colander under cold, running water until the water runs clear. Drain.

Place the rice, oil, salt, and water in a saucepan and bring to a boil. Allow the rice to boil, uncovered, until almost all of the water has evaporated, 10 to 12 minutes.

Stir the rice, cover, and reduce the heat to low. Simmer for 8 to 10 minutes.

Remove from the heat and fluff with a fork just before serving.

YIELD: APPROXIMATELY 4 CUPS

Chipotle Ketchup

This spicy, smoky condiment makes for a zingy alternative to ordinary ketchup. You can also use it as a lively substitute for tomato paste.

1/4 cup olive oil
1 onion, cut into 1/4-inch dice
3 tablespoons finely chopped garlic
3 small cans (6 ounces each) tomato paste
1 small can (3 ounces) chipotle chiles
Salt to taste

Preheat the oven to 275°.

Heat the olive oil in an ovenproof saucepan or skillet. Add the onion and garlic and sauté over medium heat for 5 to 6 minutes.

Stir in the tomato paste and chipotles, cover with a lid or aluminum foil, and place in the oven for 1 hour.

Remove from the oven and let cool. Transfer to a blender and purée until smooth. Add the salt. Keep refrigerated in an airtight container for up to 6 months.

YIELD: APPROXIMATELY 3 CUPS

Ancho Chile Mustard

This is a mustard with kick. It has a depth of flavor that makes it a lot more interesting than plain mustard.

1 teaspoon olive oil
2 tablespoons finely chopped white onion
4 dried ancho chiles, seeded, toasted, and ground (page 6)
2 teaspoons minced garlic
1 teaspoon crushed red pepper flakes
1 tablespoon Colman's dry mustard
2 tablespoons Dijon mustard
3 tablespoons sherry vinegar
1 tablespoon honey
1/3 cup mayonnaise
1/4 cup sour cream

Heat the olive oil in a skillet. Add the onion and sauté over medium-high heat for 2 to 3 minutes. Transfer the onion to a blender. Add the remaining ingredients and blend until smooth. Store refrigerated in an airtight container.

YIELD: APPROXIMATELY 1 CUP

Roasted Garlic Aïoli

Whenever you're thinking of using mayonnaise, try this recipe. It makes a wonderful sandwich spread and goes with just about everything.

3 heads roasted garlic (page 6)
2 tablespoons sherry vinegar
1 teaspoon fresh rosemary leaves
3 egg yolks, at room temperature
1 cup olive oil
Salt and pepper to taste

Preheat the oven to 450°.

Place the garlic, vinegar, rosemary, and egg yolks in a blender and purée for 30 seconds. With the machine running, add the olive oil in a slow, steady stream until emulsified. Keep refrigerated in an airtight container for up to 1 month.

YIELD: APPROXIMATELY 1 1/2 CUPS

Saffron Mayonnaise

This is an all-purpose mayo that is distinguished by its attractive yellow hue and heady saffron flavor.

1 tablespoon saffron threads
1/4 cup dry white wine
2 egg yolks, at room temperature
1 teaspoon roasted garlic (page 6)
2 tablespoons sherry vinegar
Salt to taste
1 teaspoon crushed red pepper flakes
1 cup vegetable oil

Place the saffron and wine in a saucepan and bring to a simmer over low heat. Continue to simmer for 3 minutes, or until the wine develops a deep saffron color. Remove from the heat and strain, discarding the saffron threads. Let cool completely.

Place the egg yolks, garlic, vinegar, salt, and red pepper flakes in a blender and purée for 30 seconds. With the machine still running, add the oil in a slow, steady stream until emulsified. Slowly add the saffron-infused wine and continue to blend until emulsified. Store in the refrigerator for up to 3 months.

YIELD: APPROXIMATELY 1 1/2 CUPS

STOCKS

Chicken Stock

Homemade chicken stock always has more flavor, and it's well worth the effort. Roasting the chicken bones will make a darker stock, especially if you add Annatto Oil (page 8).

4 pounds chicken bones
1 chicken (3 to 4 pounds), well rinsed, cut into 8 pieces
2 cups coarsely chopped onions
2 cloves garlic
1 cup sliced carrots
1 cup sliced celery
3 bay leaves
1 bunch thyme, tied
1 bunch parsley, tied
1 bunch dill, tied
10 to 12 black peppercorns
Salt to taste
1 gallon cold water

Rinse the chicken bones under cold running water and chop coarsely. Place all the ingredients in a large stockpot and bring to a boil. Skim off any impurities or scum that rise to the surface. Reduce the heat, and simmer partially covered for 1½ hours, replacing the water as necessary. Skim, strain, and use the same day, or let cool and freeze.

YIELD: APPROXIMATELY 1 GALLON

STOCK NOTE *If the stock is allowed to simmer too quickly, you may need to add 1 to 2 cups of additional water in order to maintain the stock's level. If a strong stock is desired, continue to cook and reduce the recipe until the desired strength is achieved.*

Demi-Glace

This is a very simple reduced veal stock that makes a great base for sauces. Ask your butcher to split the veal bones for you.

6 pounds veal knuckle bones, split
1 bottle (750 ml.) dry red wine
1 cup brandy
1 pound onions, quartered
1 head garlic, halved crosswise
1 cup sliced carrots
1 cup sliced celery
½ cup fresh thyme leaves
3 bay leaves
2 tablespoons peppercorns
½ stick cinnamon
½ star anise
1 whole clove
6 sprigs parsley
1½ gallons cold water
Salt to taste

Preheat the oven to 450°.

Place the veal bones in a large, heavy-bottomed roasting pan and roast uncovered until the bones are browned on top, about 20 minutes. Turn the bones over with tongs and continue roasting until the bones are evenly browned, about 45 minutes to 1 hour.

Remove the pan from the oven and transfer the bones to a large stockpot. Pour off the fat from the pan. Add the wine and brandy to the pan and deglaze over high heat, scraping the pan with a spatula or large spoon to loosen all the bits. Transfer the liquid to the stockpot.

Add the remaining ingredients to the stockpot, making sure to add enough water to cover the bones completely. Slowly bring the mixture to a boil over medium-low heat. Then reduce the heat, and continue simmering for at least 12 hours, adding enough cold water every 3 or 4 hours to keep the bones covered.

Strain the stock into a saucepan. Let it cool, and skim off the fat and any impurities that rise to the surface.

Bring the liquid to a boil, and allow it to reduce over high heat to about 1 quart. Let it cool before you freeze it.

YIELD: APPROXIMATELY 1 QUART

Fish Stock

I prefer to make this stock with snapper, sole, or grouper bones, or with grouper heads—my personal favorite for the best flavor. Avoid using oilier fish like salmon or kingfish, which tend to overpower the taste of the stock. Be sure to remove the gills from the fish, as they may discolor the stock.

2 tablespoons olive oil
1 cup coarsely chopped onions
1 head garlic, halved crosswise
½ cup sliced carrots
½ cup sliced celery
3 pounds fish trimmings (bones, scraps, and heads)
2 bay leaves
6 sprigs thyme
6 sprigs parsley
1 bottle (750 ml.) dry white wine
2 quarts cold water
Salt to taste

Heat the olive oil in a large skillet. Add the onions, garlic, carrots, and celery, and sauté over medium heat until vegetables are soft, about 8 to 10 minutes. Transfer the sautéed vegetables to a large stockpot, and add the remaining ingredients.

Slowly bring to a simmer, never allowing the soup to boil. Skim off any impurities or scum that rises to the surface, and simmer for 1 hour. Skim again, strain, and use the same day, or cool and freeze until needed.

YIELD: APPROXIMATELY 2 QUARTS

Lobster Stock

This recipe is a bit time-consuming, but the results are worth the extra effort. If you eat lobster frequently, save the shells and carcasses in an airtight bag in the freezer until you have enough to make a stock. A combination of lobster and shrimp shells, or just shrimp shells, may also be used.

5 pounds lobster (carcasses or shells), split
1 cup butter
4 cups coarsely chopped onions
3 heads garlic, halved crosswise
2 cups sliced carrots
2 cups sliced celery
4 bay leaves
1 bunch thyme, tied
1 bunch parsley, tied
1 tablespoon crushed red pepper flakes (optional)
3 tablespoons black peppercorns
Salt to taste
3 cups dry sherry
1/4 cup tomato paste
4 quarts water

Thoroughly wash out the halved lobster shells, taking care to remove the lungs.

Melt the butter in a heavy skillet over medium heat. Add the lobster, onions, garlic, carrots, celery, herbs, red pepper flakes, peppercorns, and salt and sauté for about 35 minutes, stirring frequently.

Add the sherry and tomato paste and cook until the alcohol evaporates, about 5 minutes.

Add the water and simmer for 2 hours, skimming off any impurities or scum that rise to the surface. Replace the water as necessary. Skim again, strain, and use the same day, or let cool and freeze until needed.

YIELD: APPROXIMATELY 1 GALLON

ADOBOS & MARINADES

Fresh Cilantro Adobo

We make large batches of this basic adobo at the restaurants. It's a good, all-purpose adobo, especially for poultry, pork, or beef, which I like to marinate at least 12 hours.

1 1/2 cups fresh cilantro (leaves and stems)
3 bay leaves
2 teaspoons ground cumin
2 teaspoons dried oregano
2 teaspoons dried thyme
2 teaspoons pepper
1 tablespoon salt
1/2 cup coarsely chopped white onion
1/4 cup coarsely chopped garlic
1 cup distilled white vinegar
1/2 cup vegetable oil

Place all the ingredients, except the vegetable oil, in a blender. Purée on high speed. Transfer the mixture to a mixing bowl and whisk in the vegetable oil.

YIELD: APPROXIMATELY 2 1/2 CUPS

Ancho Chile Adobo

This adobo is particularly suitable for poultry, giving it a nice smoky flavor. The sweet, spicy flavor of the ancho chile makes this adobo an excellent choice for shrimp and scallops as well, especially if you're going to grill them.

8 dried ancho chiles, seeded, toasted, and ground (page 6)
1 small onion, coarsely chopped
10 to 12 cloves garlic, chopped
3 canned chipotle chiles, with seeds
2 tablespoons dried rosemary
1 cup freshly squeezed orange juice
Salt and pepper to taste
1 cup extra virgin olive oil

Place the chile powder, onion, garlic, chipotle chiles, rosemary, and orange juice in a blender. Purée on high speed. Transfer to a mixing bowl and whisk in the oil. Add the salt and pepper.

Marinate poultry in the adobo for 3 to 4 hours; seafood will take half the time.

YIELD: APPROXIMATELY 3 CUPS

ADOBOS & MARINADES DEFINED

Both of these words describe much the same thing; adobo is simply the Spanish word for "marinade." The only difference between them is that marinades are usually in liquid form whereas adobos can be either wet or dry.

Marinades and adobos are important elements in Latin American cooking, and just about every type of meat or fish that I grill or sauté is prepared first in a marinade or an oil-based medium. Marinades and adobos work to enhance or provide flavor and to tenderize and preserve meats. Dry adobos are used as spice rubs or pastes.

Finally, two words of advice: To avoid any possible contamination, always marinate ingredients in the refrigerator and avoid reusing a marinade or adobo.

Dry Adobo Rub

Like marinades, dry adobos give meats flavor. I like to first coat the meat in oil and then roll it in the rub. This recipe can be used to prepare most types of meat, poultry, and even fish and vegetables for grilling.

5 tablespoons fennel seeds
5 tablespoons mustard seeds
5 tablespoon toasted cumin seeds
    (page 7)
6 dried ancho chiles, or Peruvian pancha
    chiles, seeded and coarsely chopped
6 dried guajillo chiles, seeded and
    coarsely chopped
2 tablespoons crushed red pepper flakes
6 tablespoons salt

Heat a large skillet over high heat. Place all the ingredients in the skillet and toast until they become fragrant and charred and the seeds begin to crackle, 5 to 7 minutes. Remove the skillet from the heat and let cool.

Working in batches, transfer the toasted ingredients to a spice mill or coffee grinder and grind until smooth. Store in an airtight container until needed.

YIELD: APPROXIMATELY 2 CUPS

Oriental Ginger Marinade

The Asian flavors in this recipe complement the rich tones of duck breast, chicken, or lamb, which are best when marinated overnight.

$1/2$ cup chopped gingerroot
5 cloves garlic, chopped
$1/2$ cup fresh cilantro leaves
2 tablespoons Chinese five-spice powder
1 cup soy sauce
2 tablespoons honey
$1/2$ cup toasted sesame oil

Place the gingerroot, garlic, cilantro, five-spice powder, soy sauce, and honey in a blender. Purée on high speed. Transfer the mixture to a mixing bowl and whisk in the sesame oil.

YIELD: APPROXIMATELY 2$1/2$ CUPS

Garlic and Vinegar Marinade

I created this marinade for pork, but it can also be used for preparing thin cuts of beef, like shell steaks, for panfrying.

3 tablespoons minced garlic
1 cup chopped flat-leaf parsley
1 small onion, sliced into thin rings
$1/2$ cup white wine vinegar
Salt and pepper to taste

In a mixing bowl, thoroughly combine all of the ingredients. Let the meat marinate for about 3 hours.

YIELD: APPROXIMATELY 1$1/2$ CUPS

Red Tomato Marinade

This recipe is an ideal preparation for poultry, thinly cut shell or New York strip steaks, and swordfish. Poultry and steak need 4 or 5 hours to marinate; swordfish needs about 3 hours.

1 cup vegetable oil
1 small onion, diced
8 cloves garlic, chopped
1 tablespoon paprika
$3/4$ cup tomato paste
$1/4$ cup fresh thyme leaves
1 tablespoon fresh oregano leaves
2 bay leaves
Salt and pepper to taste

In a sauté pan, heat 2 tablespoons of the vegetable oil. Sauté the onion and garlic over high heat until translucent, about 2 minutes. Stir in the paprika, and sauté for another 3 minutes.

Transfer the mixture to a blender and add the tomato paste, thyme, oregano, bay leaves, salt, and pepper. Purée on high speed.

With the machine running, add the remaining vegetable oil in a slow, steady stream until emulsified.

YIELD: APPROXIMATELY 2$1/2$ CUPS

Rum Marinade

This marinade is what I call quick! In just half an hour, its flavor will penetrate any fish. I love it with a thickly cut game fish like swordfish or tuna, and it also works well with conch, snapper, softshell crabs, or scallops. Cook the fish or seafood in a small amount of the marinade and some butter.

2 cups dark rum
7 star anise
Zest of 1 lemon
1 tablespoon honey
1 teaspoon ground cinnamon
$^{1}/_{2}$ cup fresh cilantro leaves
1 tablespoon pure vanilla extract

Place all the ingredients in a blender and pulse for 30 seconds. Pour over fish or seafood and marinate for 30 minutes.

YIELD: APPROXIMATELY 2$^{1}/_{2}$ CUPS

Fast Lime Marinade

My mother used this recipe quite a bit whenever she marinated meat, but I never thought of it as a marinade back then—I just figured that it was a part of the recipe. It's a great marinade for pork chops, pork tenderloin, as well as fish and seafood, and it works quickly, hence the name. Pork will take up to 1 hour, but you can marinate whole snapper or any type of fish effectively in just 5 to 10 minutes. Take care, for fish or seafood will "overcook" in the marinade if you leave it longer than 15 minutes.

Juice of 12 limes (about 1 cup)
3 cloves garlic, chopped
1 bay leaf
3 tablespoons chopped fresh cilantro leaves
1 tablespoon chopped fresh oregano leaves
3 tablespoons chopped fresh parsley
1 teaspoon toasted cumin (page 7)

Place all the ingredients in a blender and purée on high speed. Pour over the meat or fish and marinate for 1 hour.

YIELD: APPROXIMATELY 1$^{1}/_{2}$ CUPS

Buttermilk Marinade

This is a great marinade for liver, chicken, or fish, especially if you plan to panfry or deep-fry. The marinade will permeate the meat and keep it moist.

2 cups buttermilk
2 tablespoons chopped fresh sage leaves
2 tablespoons chopped fresh thyme leaves
$^{1}/_{2}$ cup chopped flat-leaf parsley
6 cloves garlic, chopped
3 tablespoons pepper
1 tablespoon mustard seeds

Place all the ingredients in a blender and blend well on high speed.

Marinate for a minimum of 12 hours.

YIELD: APPROXIMATELY 2$^{1}/_{2}$ CUPS

Red Wine Marinade

The robust, penetrating flavors of this marinade make it ideal for large cuts of meat like roasts or leg of lamb. Marinate the meats overnight.

$^{1}/_{2}$ tablespoon fresh rosemary leaves
$^{1}/_{2}$ tablespoon fresh oregano leaves
6 shallots, chopped
1 tablespoon Colman's dry mustard
$^{1}/_{2}$ bottle (375 ml.) dry red wine, such as Spanish Rioja
Salt and pepper to taste

Place all the ingredients in a blender and purée on high speed until smooth.

YIELD: APPROXIMATELY 2 CUPS

COCKTAILS & DRINKS

Opposite page: Mojito

THERE ARE PLENTY of rum drinks in this chapter, reflecting rum's preeminence as the liquor of choice in the Caribbean and tropical Latin America. Sugarcane is a major crop across these regions, and a significant amount is harvested and turned into molasses (the component left after the sugar has been separated out), then fermented and distilled to make rum. Sugarcane is also the source of the potent aguardiente, a popular liquor in some parts of Latin America.

Sugarcane was brought to the New World by the early Spanish explorers. Though native to Southeast Asia, sugarcane was cultivated for centuries in the Mediterranean region. Rum is recognized historically as the favorite liquor of seafarers, but its popularity spread within Europe (England and Ireland, especially) and colonial America. In fact, restrictions placed by the British on the rum trade were an indirect cause of the American Revolution.

There are sixty or more different brands of rum available (if you know where to look for them). However, the market leader, and a favorite of mine, is Bacardi rum. The Bacardi family, originally from the Catalonia province of Spain, settled in Cuba and began producing rum there in the 1860s. The invention of cocktails like the daiquiri and Cuba Libre around the turn of the century spurred sales, and over the years, the company expanded its operations to other Caribbean and South American locations. After the Cuban revolution of 1960, Bacardi shifted its headquarters to Puerto Rico. A few of my other favorite rums are C. J. Wray, from Jamaica; Pampero, from Venezuela; and Brugal, from Santa Domingo.

If you travel through South America or the Caribbean, you'll find that most of the local cocktails are made with rum, although beer and wine are also popular. One of our best-selling cocktails is the Pisco Sour, a classic Peruvian drink made with Pisco, a grape brandy that tastes somewhat like grappa. A couple of other Pisco favorites are also included here. Some of the cocktails in this chapter are made with champagne or cava, a Spanish sparkling wine.

Another major component to these recipes is the wonderful bounty of tropical fruits. With all the different rums and fruits available to you, there are unlimited combinations to try. Feel free to be creative.

Note: The recipes that follow use measurements in ounces. The standard liquor jigger is $1\frac{1}{2}$ ounces (equivalent to 3 tablespoons), but they're also available in 1- and 2-ounce sizes.

The Original Daiquiri

This is the original version of the daiquiri. It is said to have been created about 100 years ago by Jennings Cox, a copper mine engineer who worked in a village called Daiquiri, just outside Santiago in Cuba. The cocktail was popularized by Havana's La Floridita ("Little Florida") bar, and became a legend once Ernest Hemingway discovered it there. (This was his favorite cocktail.) The recipe calls for fresh lime juice, and that's the only way to make it. A word of caution: This is a thirst-quenching drink; its effect can creep up on you!

2 ounces white rum

1 ounce freshly squeezed lime juice

$1/2$ teaspoon sugar

$1/4$ cup crushed ice

1 lime slice, for garnish

Place the rum, lime juice, sugar, and ice in a blender and blend until smooth. Pour into a daiquiri or hurricane glass and garnish with the lime slice.

YIELD: 1 COCKTAIL

Mojito

Mojito, a variation of the word mojar, means "to wet" in Spanish—an appropriate description of this cocktail. This is my version of another classic Cuban drink created at La Floridita that, like the daiquiri, met with Papa Hemingway's approval. At the restaurants, I use 7-Up instead of the traditional soda water and fresh sugarcane juice instead of sugar because of its flavor. Unfortunately, sugarcane juice is difficult to find unless you live in cities like Miami or New York. Pictured on page 14.

$1/4$ cup fresh sugarcane juice, or
   1 teaspoon sugar

$1^1/2$ ounces light rum

4 or 5 mint leaves

Crushed ice

7-Up to taste

1 stick sugarcane for garnish

1 slice lime, for garnish

Place the sugarcane juice, rum, and mint leaves in a cocktail shaker and stir. (If using sugar, shake vigorously until the sugar dissolves.)

Fill a tall rocks glass with crushed ice and pour the cocktail over the ice. Add the 7-Up and stir gently. Garnish with the sugarcane stick and serve.

YIELD: 1 COCKTAIL

Cortadito

This drink was invented by my mother, whose favorite cocktail was a White Russian. One evening, when my mom was about to make a White Russian, she was seized by the Cocktail Muse and made this drink instead. It turned out great!

1 ounce Kahlua

$1/2$ ounce light rum

$1/2$ ounce freshly brewed espresso,
   cooled

2 ounces evaporated milk

1 teaspoon sugar

Crushed ice

Whipped cream, for garnish

Place the Kahlua, rum, coffee, milk, and sugar in a cocktail shaker. Shake vigorously. Fill a rocks glass with crushed ice and pour the cocktail over the ice. Garnish with the whipped cream and serve.

YIELD: 1 COCKTAIL

Guavalada

In this recipe, I've taken the traditional piña colada and substituted guava for the pineapple. If you omit the alcohol, it also makes a very good "virgin" drink. In fact, that's the way it was created. My father, a big fan of milkshakes, used to make guava shakes at home all the time. One day he added some coconut milk, and I took this idea and added rum to make a robust frozen cocktail. I assure you that you'll like the taste of guava and coconut together. It's a combination that could become a classic. You can buy canned guava marmalade in Latin markets.

2 ounces dark rum

1 ounce light rum

2 ounces Coco Lopez

1 ounce (2 tablespoons) guava marmalade
   or canned guava nectar

$^1/_4$ cup crushed ice

Shaved coconut, for garnish

Place all the ingredients together in a blender and blend until smooth. Pour into a hurricane glass and garnish with the coconut.

YIELD: 1 COCKTAIL

Coquito Rico

I was inspired to make this cocktail during a trip to Puerto Rico. Serving it in green coconut shells makes a very dramatic presentation, but if you can't get green coconuts, you can make do with brown ones. (The brown shells are smaller than the green ones, so this recipe will yield more servings if you use them.) This isn't an easy drink to prepare at home, but trust me—it's a terrific summer cocktail that'll evoke the tropics.

4 green coconuts

$^1/_4$ cup freshly squeezed lime juice

Dash of angostura bitters

1 cup Malibu coconut-flavored rum

1 cup dark rum

$^1/_4$ cup crushed ice

4 lime wedges, for garnish

Whack off the top of the coconuts with a large cleaver. Pour the coconut juice into a bowl and reserve.

Make 2 drinks at a time by placing $^1/_2$ cup of the reserved coconut juice in a large cocktail shaker. In a separate container, mix the remaining ingredients together and add half to the shaker. Shake vigorously.

Pour the mixture into the coconut shells, add a lime wedge to the cocktail for garnish, and serve with straws. Repeat for the remaining 2 cocktails.

YIELD: 4 COCKTAILS

Miami Wami

Chocolate lovers will really appreciate this one. The sweetness of the crème de cacao balances the tartness of the fruit juice. Another great cocktail. Drink it up!

2 ounces dark rum

1 ounce crème de cacao

1 ounce sweetened condensed milk

1 ounce freshly squeezed grapefruit juice

6 ice cubes

$^1/_2$ teaspoon shaved bittersweet chocolate,
   for garnish

Place all the ingredients in a blender and blend until smooth. Pour into martini glasses, garnish with the shaved chocolate, and serve immediately.

YIELD: 1 COCKTAIL

Chicama Colada

This thirst-quenching cocktail is a spin on the piña colada that's made with passion fruit juice instead of pineapple juice. The sweet-tart flavor of the passion fruit and the richness of the coconut forge a great combination of flavors. You'll love it.

$^1/_2$ cup frozen unsweetened
    passion fruit concentrate
2 ounces Coco Lopez
2 ounces light rum
I ounce dark rum
$^1/_2$ cup crushed ice
Shaved coconut, for garnish

Place all the ingredients in a blender and blend until smooth. Pour into a hurricane glass and garnish with the coconut.

YIELD: 1 COCKTAIL

Banana-Ginger Fling

I made this frozen cocktail after a Chinese company sent a sample to me of a new ginger liqueur called Canton. I really enjoyed the flavor, and figured that it might go nicely with bananas, lime juice, and rum. Are there any cocktails worth drinking that aren't made with rum?

I$^1/_2$ ounces light rum
$^1/_3$ ripe banana, peeled
$^1/_2$ ounce freshly squeezed lime juice
I teaspoon sugar
I ounce Canton (ginger liqueur)
$^1/_2$ cup crushed ice
I banana slice, for garnish

Place all the ingredients in a blender and purée. Pour into a tall glass and garnish with the banana slice.

YIELD: 1 COCKTAIL

The Rumm-Ba

Here's another rum creation of mine, inspired by the dance the rumba. It's enough to make you want to shake your hips and take to the dance floor, especially after two or three cocktails!

I ounce light rum
$^1/_2$ ounce banana liqueur
Splash of Rose's Lime Juice
$^1/_2$ ounce grenadine syrup
Crushed ice
I orange slice, for garnish
I maraschino cherry, for garnish

Place the rum, banana liqueur, lime juice, and grenadine in a cocktail shaker. Shake vigorously. Fill a highball glass with ice and pour the cocktail over the ice. Garnish with the orange slice and cherry.

YIELD: 1 COCKTAIL

Tamarind Sour

Tamarind grows inside pods that you break open to reveal small seedpods that almost look like dates. You need to soak the fruit in water to release the tart-tasting brown pulp. (You can buy the canned tamarind juice called for in this recipe in Latin markets.) I cooked up the pulp and experimented by mixing it with some Southern Comfort in a blender. After picking some herbs in the garden for a pasta dish, we relaxed with these delicious cocktails—it's funny how a cocktail can trigger wonderful memories and evoke vivid pictures in one's mind.

I ounce Southern Comfort
Dash of Rose's Lime Juice
$^1/_2$ ounce grenadine syrup
$^1/_2$ tablespoon sugar
2 ounces canned tamarind juice
Crushed ice

Place the Southern Comfort, lime juice, grenadine, sugar, and tamarind juice in a cocktail shaker. Shake vigorously. Fill a highball glass with crushed ice and pour the cocktail over the ice.

YIELD: 1 COCKTAIL

Mangini

This champagne-mango cocktail is a play on words on the peach-based Bellini, which was invented by Harry Cipriani at Harry's Bar in Venice, Italy. I like to think of the Mangini as an improvement, and it makes a great Sunday brunch cocktail. The mango purée can be stored for a day or two in the refrigerator. You can substitute frozen mango if fresh is unavailable, but as always, fresh is best.

2 very ripe mangoes
$^1/_2$ to 1 cup ice water, as needed
1 bottle champagne or cava, chilled

Peel the mangoes and cut away the flesh from the pits. Place the flesh in a food processor and purée until smooth. If the purée is too thick, slowly add some of the ice water until the desired consistency is reached.

In the bottom of each champagne flute glass place 1 ounce of the mango purée and top off with your favorite champagne.

YIELD: 6 COCKTAILS

Mamey Margarita

Mamey is a large tropical fruit with a very aromatic, sweet flavor. Frank, the bartender at Yuca, invented this cocktail on one occasion when we had an excessive amount of mamey in the kitchen. It turned out to be a hit, and it's a recipe I use to this day at my restaurants. The coarsely textured kosher salt is a must for this recipe.

1 $^1/_2$ ounces Cuervo gold or your
    favorite tequila
$^1/_2$ ounce Cointreau
3 ounces freshly squeezed lime juice
1 ounce grenadine syrup
1 $^1/_2$ ounces fresh or frozen mamey purée
Coarse kosher salt
1 lime wedge
Ice cubes
1 lime slice or mamey slice, for garnish

Place the tequila, Cointreau, lime juice, grenadine, and mamey purée in a cocktail shaker. Shake vigorously.

Place the salt in a shallow saucer or on a plate. Wet the rim of a margarita glass with the lime wedge and dip the rim in the salt. Fill the glass with ice cubes and pour the cocktail over the ice. Garnish with a slice of lime.

To make a frozen mamey margarita, place the tequila, Cointreau, lime juice, grenadine, mamey purée, and ice in a blender and blend well. Garnish with a slice of mamey.

YIELD: 1 COCKTAIL

Cuba Libre

Literally meaning "Free Cuba," this cocktail dates back to the Spanish-American War of 1898, when Cuba gained independence from Spanish rule. The drink became very popular with American soldiers fighting the war, and soon became a classic.

1 $^1/_2$ ounces dark rum
Ice cubes
Coca-Cola
1 lime wedge
1 lime slice, for garnish

Pour the rum into a tall glass. Add some ice and fill with Coca-Cola. Squeeze the lime wedge into the cocktail and garnish the glass with the slice of lime.

YIELD: 1 COCKTAIL

Opposite page: Mangini

Mulatto Cubano

Mulatto means "half black, half white," and this drink has that kind of coloring. I've adapted it from the classic Cuban drink of the same name and from the drink my Cuban parents made for me with Coca-Cola and evaporated milk or with malta, a carbonated malt-flavored drink. (I think it was considered a super-medicinal kid's drink, but it sure kept us pumped up with sugar.) Licor 43 comes from Spain, and has a distinctive licorice flavor.

$1/2$ ounce Licor 43
$1/2$ ounce crème de cacao
1 ounce evaporated milk
Ice cubes
Coca-Cola

Place the Licor 43, crème de cacao, and evaporated milk in a cocktail shaker. Shake vigorously. Fill a rocks glass with ice and pour the cocktail over the ice. Top off the glass with Coca-Cola.

YIELD: 1 COCKTAIL

Pisco Sour

This is a classic South American drink made with Pisco, a grape liqueur similar to grappa. We sell a lot of these at the restaurants. You'll find different variations if you travel from country to country in South America, as the local Pisco and the recipe change, but the most important thing is to use fresh lime juice. Whereas some people like to sprinkle cinnamon over the top, others prefer a splash of bitters, which is how I like it. If you can't find Pisco, substitute grappa.

$1^1/_2$ ounces Pisco
1 egg white
1 teaspoon superfine sugar
2 tablespoons freshly squeezed lime juice
8 to 10 ice cubes
Splash of angostura bitters

Place the Pisco, egg white, sugar, lime juice, and ice in a cocktail shaker. Shake vigorously. Strain into a martini glass and add the bitters. Serve immediately.

YIELD: 1 COCKTAIL

Pisco Martini

This is the macho Latin American version of the classic martini—shaken, not stirred.

1 lime wedge
3 ounces Pisco or grappa
Ice cubes
Splash of dry vermouth
1 pitted kalamata olive, for garnish

Rub the rim of a martini glass with the lime wedge. Place the Pisco, ice, and vermouth in a cocktail shaker. Shake vigorously. Strain into the martini glass and garnish with the olive and lime wedge.

YIELD: 1 COCKTAIL

Morir Soñando

The name of this frozen cocktail means, literally, "to die, dreaming," which is a Spanish saying that's the equivalent of "dying and going to heaven." It seemed appropriate when I named it, and I'm sure you'll agree when you taste it.

3 ounces Pisco or grappa
1 ounce triple sec or Cointreau
2 ounces evaporated milk
2 ounces freshly squeezed orange juice
1 teaspoon pure vanilla extract
2 teaspoons sugar
Crushed ice
1 orange slice, for garnish

Place the Pisco, triple sec, evaporated milk, orange juice, vanilla, sugar, and ice in a blender and blend until smooth. Pour into a tall glass and garnish with the orange slice.

YIELD: 1 COCKTAIL

Champagne Sangría

This makes an excellent drink for summer entertaining; if you have some friends over, this cocktail will surely impress them. It's inspired by the Spanish sangría, which is usually made with red wine. I've always liked to make my sangría somewhat unusual, mixing fruit with sparkling wine or champagne to make a white sangría. When they're in season, mangoes and peaches are ideal, because their flavors combine perfectly with the champagne and don't overwhelm it. Apples or pears make good alternatives, but avoid fruit with strong flavors, such as pineapple or cantaloupe. (You can prepare the fruit ahead of time, but add the champagne at the last minute or you'll lose the bubbles.)

1 semi-ripe mango, peeled, pitted, and sliced
2 peaches, peeled, pitted, and sliced
3 limes, sliced
2 lemons, sliced
1 orange, sliced
1 cup seedless green grapes
$^1/_2$ cup Cointreau
1 bottle champagne or cava, chilled

Place all the sliced fruit and the grapes in a large punchbowl. Pour the Cointreau over the fruit and toss gently. Just before serving, add the chilled champagne and stir gently. Serve the wine with some of the fruit in large chilled wine glasses.

Note: You can use any leftover fruit for a tasty fruit salad. Just make sure the kids don't get to it first!

YIELD: 6 COCKTAILS

Tisana

This Venezuelan champagne cocktail is great for brunch. My first encounter with it was at a hotel bar in Caracas. The bartender who recommended it told me that they also made a nonalcoholic version using apple cider, which is an option for kids or adults. Tisana makes a delicious light punch for a large party.

2 cups canned pineapple juice, chilled
2 cups freshly squeezed orange juice, chilled
1 can (10 ounces) peaches in heavy syrup
2 green apples, peeled, cored, and coarsely chopped
2 tablespoons sugar
1 teaspoon ground nutmeg
2 teaspoons angostura bitters
1 bottle cava or sparkling apple cider, chilled

Place one half of the pineapple and orange juice in a blender. Add the peaches with only a small amount of the syrup and the apples, sugar, nutmeg, and bitters. Purée until smooth.

Transfer the mixture to a decorative pitcher. Add the remaining juices and stir well. Store in the refrigerator until ready to use.

Just before serving, slowly add the champagne, stir gently, and serve in chilled wine glasses.

YIELD: 10 COCKTAILS

Passion Fruit– Champagne Cocktail

What a great combination—two aphrodisiacs together, some would say. This is another ideal cocktail for Sunday brunch or for summertime entertaining. Taste the passion fruit to make sure that it's not too acidic (if it is, its sharpness will overwhelm the champagne). Add some sugar if necessary.

3 passion fruit, halved
1 bottle champagne or cava, chilled
$^3/_4$ cup unsweetened passion fruit juice, chilled

Scoop out the seeds, pulp, and juice from the passion fruit and place them in a small bowl. Pour approximately 5 ounces of champagne into each flute glass. Evenly divide the passion fruit seeds and pulp between the glasses, and add 1 ounce of the passion fruit juice to each. Swirl gently to activate the bubbles.

YIELD: 6 COCKTAILS

CHIPS & BREADS

Opposite page: Yellow Arepas

CHIPS AND BREADS are important elements of Latin American cuisine, and every country has its own versions of them. Chips make great snacks, and the recipes in this chapter are so versatile, they can be used with any of the salsas in the next chapter. At some time or another we serve all the chips in this chapter at my restaurants, although we sometimes vary the seasonings. (One perennial on the menu is the plantain chips, which we always season with garlic.)

Always keep in mind Rule Numero Uno for deep-frying chips: *Never* leave the hot oil in the pan unattended. See pages 6 and 7 for other tips that will be helpful when making the recipes in this chapter.

Nuevo Latino cuisine draws upon a rich and varied heritage of breads. The "staff of life" plays an all-too-significant role in the diet of many who live in the poorer Latin American countries.

Breads are served with breakfast, with soups, with dinner, and they're used for sandwiches and snacks.

Many people think of bread as a European invention, but long before the Spanish introduced wheat bread to the New World, different types of breads were made from tubers such as yuca, boniato, and malanga in various parts of the Caribbean and Central and South America. It is still common there to find breads made from these tubers, sometimes with the addition of cheese to make the texture softer and chewier as well as rich and flavorful.

Although many of the bread recipes in this chapter are faithful re-creations of Latin American recipes, some are my own variations. The breads we use most to accompany our food are the Yellow Arepas, the Pan d Bono, the Garlic Boniato Bread, and the Cuban Corn Bread.

Cumin Boniato Chips

I usually succeed in stumping people with these chips, because they really don't know what they are. Boniato, or Cuban sweet potatoes, crisp up well for these chips, which are unexpectedly sweet when you bite into them. Because they have a higher sugar content, they'll brown more quickly than regular potato chips. For best results, use a mandoline slicer to cut the boniato. These chips should keep in an airtight container for 2 to 3 days.

Toasted cumin to taste (page 7)

3 cups canola oil

2 large boniatos, peeled and finely
    sliced lengthwise

Salt to taste

Grind the cumin in a coffee grinder. Set aside.

Heat the oil to 350° in a deep fryer or heavy-bottomed saucepan. Immediately add the boniato slices one at a time, but do not overload the pan or the oil will not stay hot enough. (Cook in batches if necessary.) Deep-fry until golden, 3 to 4 minutes.

Remove the chips with a wire-mesh strainer and drain on paper towels. Sprinkle with the salt and cumin and let cool.

YIELD: 4 SERVINGS

Lemon-Cayenne Yuca Chips

These chips are seasoned with a lemon-cayenne powder, but you can substitute chile molido or ancho chile powder. However, it's important that you use a pure chile powder like chile molido rather than commercial chile powders, which will invariably contain ingredients (such as salt and spices) that you don't want or need. Use a mandoline slicer, if possible, to slice the yuca, and keep the yuca in water after slicing them to extract some of the starch.

Zest of 4 lemons, finely minced

2 teaspoons salt

1 teaspoon ground cayenne pepper

3 cups canola oil

2 large yucas, peeled, finely sliced, rinsed,
    and patted dry

To dry out the lemon zest, place it on a baking sheet and leave it in the oven overnight, if you have a gas oven, with just the pilot light on. If you have an electric oven, keep it on its minimum setting until the zest is dry. Transfer the zest to a spice or coffee grinder, add the salt and cayenne, and grind to a fine powder.

Heat the oil to 350° in a deep fryer or heavy-bottomed saucepan. Immediately add the yuca chips one at a time, but do not overload the pan or the oil will not stay hot enough. (Cook in batches if necessary.) Deep-fry until golden, 3 to 4 minutes.

Remove the chips with a wire-mesh strainer and drain on paper towels. Dust chips lightly with the lemon-cayenne powder and let them cool before serving.

YIELD: 4 SERVINGS

Garlic Plantain Chips

The garlic flavoring gives these plantain chips an intriguing and unusual twist. Like the boniato chips, the plantains should be sliced with a mandoline slicer.

3 cups canola oil

2 green plantains, peeled and finely
    sliced lengthwise

Salt to taste

Garlic powder to taste

Heat the oil to 350° in a deep fryer or heavy-bottomed saucepan. Immediately add the plantain chips one at a time, but do not overload the pan or the oil will not stay hot enough. (Cook in batches if necessary.) Deep-fry until golden, 3 to 4 minutes.

Remove the chips with a wire-mesh strainer and drain on paper towels. Sprinkle with the salt and garlic powder and let cool.

YIELD: 4 SERVINGS

Red Malanga Chips

This is another recipe that confounds the casual muncher. Because the yellow malanga slices are dyed with beet juice before frying, they're not easy to identify. These chips crisp really well, and make a great snack. For a fancier presentation, I sometimes cut the malanga into triangles, rounds, or other shapes.

2 large fresh beets
1½ pounds malanga, peeled
3 cups canola oil
Salt to taste

With an electric juicer, juice the beets.

Thinly slice the malanga, preferably using a mandoline slicer, and arrange in a single layer in the bottom of a large, shallow dish. Pour some of the beet juice over the slices. Continue layering and pouring the beet juice over until you have used up the ingredients.

Heat the oil to 350° in a deep fryer or heavy-bottomed saucepan. Drain the malanga chips, then quickly add them to the oil one at a time, making sure they're not dripping with the beet juice, causing them to splatter. Do not overload the pan or the oil will not stay hot enough. (Cook in batches if necessary.)

Deep-fry until the chips look firm, 3 to 4 minutes. Remove the chips with a wire-mesh strainer and drain on paper towels. Sprinkle with salt and let cool.

YIELD: 4 SERVINGS

Patacones

This is a traditional Colombian recipe. You can peel the plantains ahead of time—they'll keep for several days if they're covered well in the refrigerator. You can cut the rolled-out plantains to any size you want. Use these thick plantain chips to accompany dips or salsas.

Canola oil, for deep-frying
6 large green plantains, peeled (page 7)

Heat the oil to 350° in a deep fryer or heavy-bottomed skillet. Fry one plantain at a time until golden brown, about 15 minutes. Remove from the oil with a slotted spoon, drain on paper towels, and let cool.

Place a damp kitchen towel on a flat work surface and lay a plantain on the towel. Fold half of the towel over to cover the plantain. Using a rolling pin, roll out the covered plantain as you would pie dough, to a thickness of ¼ inch.

Transfer the plantain carefully onto plastic wrap. Roll out the remaining plantains, layering them on top of each other when flat, separated with plastic wrap. Leave the plantains rolled out or cut them into chips or different shapes.

Reheat ½ inch of the canola oil in the skillet and fry the plantains until crisp, 3 to 5 minutes. Drain on paper towels.

YIELD: 6 SERVINGS

Rice Cakes

This is an ideal way to use up leftover rice—it's almost like making potato pancakes, only with rice. These cakes can be served by themselves or with black beans, but they go particularly well topped with some sour cream and served with Gloria's Black Bean Soup (page 70). I know you'll enjoy them.

1 onion, coarsely chopped
3 cups cooked day-old rice
½ cup all-purpose flour
¼ cup finely chopped chives
2 tablespoons finely chopped
  fresh thyme leaves
¼ cup finely chopped fresh parsley
1 large tomato, seeded and chopped
3 eggs, beaten
¼ cup heavy cream
1 teaspoon salt
½ teaspoon pepper
2 cups vegetable oil

Place the onion in a food processor and finely grind. Transfer the onion to a large mixing bowl and add the rice, flour, herbs, tomato, eggs, cream, salt, and pepper. Mix together to form a lumpy batter.

In a shallow pan, heat 1 cup of the oil over high heat. Spoon in half the batter, 2 tablespoons at a time, to form the cakes. Fry until golden brown, about 2 minutes per side. Drain on paper towels. Add the remaining 1 cup of oil, and repeat for the remaining batter. These cakes can also be cooked on a griddle lightly coated with cooking spray if you want to reduce the fat content. Serve 2 rice cakes per person.

YIELD: 10 RICE CAKES

Cuban Bread

My father loves bread, and when I was growing up in Manhattan, I'd often go with him on his frequent trips to the bakery that his cousin Cachita owned. I enjoyed the wonderful aromas of freshly baked bread. There's nothing like a slice of the real thing, warm from the oven, with a cup of steaming café con leche.

1/3 cup vegetable shortening

1 teaspoon salt

1 tablespoon sugar

1 1/2 cups hot water

2 packages active dry yeast

6 cups bread flour

1/2 cup cornmeal

In a large bowl, combine the vegetable shortening, salt, sugar, and hot water with an electric mixer (or by hand) until the shortening melts. Let the mixture cool to at least 110°. Stir in the yeast and let the mixture proof for 5 to 10 minutes.

Add the flour, 1 cup at a time, and slowly mix with the dough hook attachment (or by hand) until the dough no longer sticks to the bowl, 5 to 8 minutes.

Transfer the dough to a lightly oiled or buttered bowl, cover the bowl with plastic wrap, and let the dough rise in a warm place until doubled in volume, about 1 1/2 hours.

Punch down the dough and turn it over. Cover the bowl and let the dough rise for 1 1/2 hours.

Punch down the dough and turn it out onto a lightly floured work surface. Divide the dough in half and shape into loaves. Sprinkle a baking sheet with the cornmeal, place the loaves on top, and cover with plastic wrap. Let the loaves rise for 30 minutes.

Preheat the oven to 400°.

Uncover the loaves and brush them with warm water. Bake for 25 minutes.

Remove the baking sheet from the oven and brush the loaves again with warm water. Reduce the heat to 350° and bake until lightly browned, about 25 minutes.

Remove the bread from the oven and turn out onto wire racks to cool.

YIELD: 2 LOAVES

Garlic Boniato Bread

Boniato makes a delicious potato bread, adding a sweeter flavor than regular potatoes. When cooking the garlic, remember that the browner it gets, the more flavor it will lend to the bread. Try putting a little butter on a hot slice straight out of the oven—absolutely fantastic. There are times when I just can't wait for it to get cool enough to handle!

1 boniato, peeled and cut into 1/2-inch dice

2 packages active dry yeast

1/2 cup lukewarm water

1/4 cup sugar

3 tablespoons melted butter

1 teaspoon salt

2 eggs

3 1/2 to 4 cups all-purpose flour

1/2 tablespoon olive oil

6 cloves garlic, minced

Bring a small pan of salted water to a boil and cook the boniato for 15 minutes. Strain and mash in a bowl.

While the boniato is cooking, sprinkle the yeast over the warm water in a mixing bowl. Add 1 teaspoon of the sugar, stir, and let proof for 5 to 10 minutes.

Add 1/2 cup mashed boniato, the remaining sugar, the melted butter, salt, and eggs, and mix together until thoroughly incorporated. With an electric mixer on low, mix in 1 1/2 cups of the flour. Add the remaining flour in small increments until a stiff dough forms. Cover the bowl with plastic wrap and let the dough rise in a warm place for 1 1/2 hours.

Heat the olive oil in a skillet. Sauté the garlic over high heat until browned, 3 to 5 minutes. Punch down the dough and vigorously stir in the garlic. Transfer the dough to a 9-inch round cake pan. Cover, and let the dough rise again until doubled in volume, about 1 hour.

Preheat the oven to 375°. Bake until brown, 35 to 45 minutes.

Remove the bread from the oven and turn out onto a wire rack to cool.

YIELD: 1 LOAF

Inca Bread

This is a terrific quick bread along the lines of Southwestern Indian fry bread. This one's named after the advanced South American civilization encountered by the Spanish. When Julia Child ate it at Yuca, she asked for seconds and thirds, and said she could tell it was cooked in lard straight away. Yes, that's Julia Child.

2 cups all-purpose flour
1 cup whole-wheat flour
2 teaspoons baking powder
1 teaspoon salt
1½ cups milk
1 to 2 pounds lard, for frying

In a mixing bowl, thoroughly combine the flours, baking powder, salt, and milk to form a dough. Transfer to a lightly floured work surface and knead until smooth, about 5 to 8 minutes.

Place the dough in a lightly oiled bowl. Roll the dough around until it is covered with the oil. Cover the bowl with plastic wrap and let the dough rest in a warm place for 20 minutes.

Divide the dough into 2 to 3-ounce pieces and roll them out into irregular shapes (ovals, ellipses, long thin forms, and so on), about ⅛-inch thick.

In a heavy-bottomed skillet, heat the lard over high heat. (There should be about 2 inches of melted lard.) Place the dough shapes in the hot oil and fry until browned, 1 to 2 minutes per side.

YIELD: 1 DOZEN BREADS

Orange Cumin Bread

A wonderful bread for Christmas and the holiday season. It's almost dessert-like with the flavors of orange and cumin, and Bijol, a food coloring that's available at Latin groceries, gives the bread an extraterrestrial appearance! Some people think it's a rye bread and they're not convinced even when they taste the cumin seeds. I like to serve this bread with olive oil, because the bread soaks it up really well. It makes great toast and is perfect for an egg and bacon breakfast sandwich.

1 package active dry yeast
¼ cup lukewarm water
1 tablespoon sugar
1 cup freshly squeezed orange juice
1 teaspoon salt
3 tablespoons melted butter
3 tablespoons grated orange zest
3 to 3½ cups all-purpose flour
2 tablespoons cumin seeds
1 tablespoon water
1 egg white
1 teaspoon Bijol (optional)

Sprinkle the yeast over the warm water in a mixing bowl and add 1 teaspoon of the sugar. Stir, and let proof for 5 to 10 minutes.

Add the rest of the sugar, the orange juice, salt, butter, and zest to the bowl. With an electric mixer, mix in 3 cups of the flour to form a stiff dough, adding more flour if necessary. Turn the dough out onto a lightly floured work surface and knead until no longer sticky, about 8 to 10 minutes. Place in a lightly oiled or buttered bowl, and lightly butter the top of the dough. Cover the bowl with plastic wrap and let the dough rise in a warm place until doubled in volume, about 1½ hours.

Butter 2 loaf pans and set aside.

Punch down the dough, then turn it out onto a lightly floured work surface. Knead the dough again for 3 minutes, adding a few cumin seeds at a time. Shape into 2 small loaves and place in the loaf pans. Cover and let rise for about 30 minutes.

Preheat the oven to 400°.

In a mixing bowl, whisk together the water, egg white, and Bijol. Brush this egg wash on top of each loaf and bake the loaves for 15 minutes.

Reduce the heat to 350° and bake the loaves until they're brown and sound hollow when tapped, about 20 minutes.

Remove the bread from the oven and turn out onto wire racks to cool.

YIELD: 2 LOAVES

Pan d Bono

This is a great cheese bread recipe from Colombia. We serve these rolls with an aji (spicy chile) dip. The yuca flour may be hard to find (see the source list on page 164), but unfortunately there are no substitutions. (Yuca flour has a texture that's rather like cornstarch, which is not surprising when you know how starchy the root vegetable is.)

These little breads freeze very well, and after you've defrosted them, they microwave better than ever—in fact, that's how I like them best, nice and chewy rather than crusty. (While baking, watch them carefully, because they can burn on the bottom even when they're just browned on the top.)

1 pound yuca flour
1 pound mozzarella cheese, grated
5 eggs
$^1/_2$ cup milk
2 tablespoons sugar
Pinch salt

Preheat the oven to 450°.

In a mixing bowl, combine the flour, cheese, eggs, milk, sugar, and salt with an electric mixer. Roll the dough into little rounds the size of golf balls and place about 3 inches apart on a greased and floured baking sheet.

Bake until golden brown, 12 to 15 minutes. Remove the bread from the oven and turn out onto wire racks to cool.

YIELD: 1 DOZEN ROLLS

Sweet Onion Flatbread

This is a very simple recipe that's ideal for cold winter days. The bread should be eaten as soon as you've made it, not only because it's more delicious that way but also because it doesn't keep well. It's good with cheese and wine. Just thinking about it makes me hungry.

1 package active dry yeast
2 cups lukewarm water
1 teaspoon sugar
6 cups all-purpose flour, sifted
1$^1/_2$ teaspoons salt
2 tablespoons extra virgin olive oil
1 cup butter
4 cups thinly sliced onions

In a mixing bowl, sprinkle the yeast over the warm water and add the sugar. Stir, and let proof for 5 to 10 minutes.

Add 4 cups of the flour and the salt and stir well to make a thick batter. Cover the bowl with a damp cloth and let it sit in a warm place until the mixture becomes frothy, about 30 minutes.

With the electric mixer dough hook (or by hand), mix the batter for 5 minutes, slowly adding the oil.

Turn the dough out onto a lightly floured work surface. Using as much of the remaining 2 cups of flour as necessary, knead the dough until it becomes satiny and slightly wrinkled, about 10 minutes.

Shape the dough into a ball and place it in a lightly oiled or buttered bowl. Cover the bowl with plastic wrap and let the dough rise in a warm place until it has doubled in volume, about 1$^1/_2$ hours.

In a sauté pan, melt the butter over medium heat. Sauté the onions until well browned, then set them aside to cool for 15 to 20 minutes.

Punch down the dough, turn it out onto a lightly floured work surface, and knead for 5 minutes. Divide the dough into 8 pieces, shape the pieces into balls, and then roll out the balls into 8-inch rounds or irregular shapes. Sprinkle each with some flour and cover with a damp towel. Let the dough rest for 20 minutes.

Preheat the oven to 500°.

Spread the browned onions out on top of each round and place the rounds on a lightly floured baking sheet. Bake until brown, about 8 minutes.

YIELD: 8 BREADS

Cuban Corn Bread

This recipe is different from the usual "quick" corn breads. Instead of making a batter, you prepare a starter, and then proof the dough. The fresh corn makes this a nice crunchy bread with a crusty top and a soft interior.

I tablespoon extra virgin olive oil
1½ cups fresh sweet corn kernels
I cup water
1¾ teaspoons salt
⅓ cup coarse cornmeal
I cup all-purpose flour

Starter

I teaspoon active dry yeast
¼ cup lukewarm water
I teaspoon honey
I cup all-purpose flour

Egg Wash

I egg
I teaspoon water

Heat the olive oil in a saucepan and sauté the corn over high heat for 5 minutes. Add the water and ¾ teaspoon of the salt, and bring the mixture to a boil. Slowly add the cornmeal, stirring constantly, and cook over medium heat or until the water is absorbed, about 10 minutes. Remove the pan from the heat and transfer to a bowl to cool.

To prepare the starter, place the yeast and warm water in a mixing bowl and let proof for about 10 minutes. Add the honey and stir until it dissolves. Stir in the cooled corn mixture.

Add the flour and mix until thoroughly incorporated. (The mixture will be a very wet batter.) Cover the bowl with plastic wrap and let the batter rise in a warm place until doubled in size, 3 to 4 hours.

When the starter has doubled, thoroughly mix in the remaining salt. Gently fold in the I cup of flour until incorpo-rated, and knead for 8 to 10 minutes (the dough will be moist but will become satiny).

Shape the dough into a loaf, cover, and let rise until doubled in volume, about I hour.

Preheat the oven to 400°.

Beat the egg and water together in a bowl. Liberally sprinkle two 9-inch loaf pans with cornmeal. Divide the dough in half and place it in the prepared pans. Brush the dough with the egg wash. Bake until golden brown, 35 to 40 minutes. Remove the bread from the oven and turn out onto wire racks to cool.

YIELD: 2 LOAVES

Yellow Arepas

Although arepas are commonly made in Venezuela as well as Colombia, this is a Colombian cheese corn cake recipe. The first time I tried them, at a Miami street fair, I knew they were the most delicious corn cakes I'd ever tasted. Arepas come in many differ-ent styles—made with white corn, yellow corn, or sweet corn, for example. These are somewhat on the sweet side, and the melted cheese gives them a wonderful crust. They're absolutely heavenly, and if there is one recipe you must make from this book, this is it. I use thawed frozen corn in this recipe because it usually contains very little starch; young, fresh corn has similar qualities and will work equally well. For best results, process the corn using a meat grinder; there really isn't a good substitute. Pictured on page 24.

2 pounds frozen yellow corn kernels, thawed
1½ cups precooked extra-fine yellow cornmeal
9 ounces mozzarella cheese, grated
2 tablespoons milk
1½ cups sugar
Pinch salt

With a meat grinder, coarsely grind the corn and place it in a mixing bowl. Add the cornmeal, cheese, milk, sugar, and salt, and mix thoroughly with an electric mixer.

Using a 1½ or 3-inch ring mold, form the mixture into about 12 large or 24 small patties. Stack them on a lightly greased baking sheet with parchment paper between them. Refrigerate for 30 minutes.

Lightly butter a griddle or heavy skillet. Cook the arepas over medium-low heat until brown, about 3 minutes per side.

YIELD: 1 DOZEN LARGE OR 2 DOZEN SMALL CORN CAKES

Plantain Bread

Plantains are close relatives of bananas, so it should come as no surprise that this recipe yields results similar to banana bread, but not quite as sweet. I like to make this bread whenever I have some leftover ripe plantains, especially when they're too ripe to make anything else. When shopping for plantains select ones with black skins, which means they're ripe.

4¹/₂ cups all-purpose flour

1 tablespoon baking soda

¹/₂ teaspoon salt

1¹/₂ cups butter, at room temperature

3 cups sugar

6 eggs

¹/₂ cup sour cream

2 teaspoons pure vanilla extract

1 teaspoon dark rum

3 cups mashed ripe plantains

Sift the flour, baking soda, and salt into a mixing bowl and set aside.

In another bowl, cream the butter and sugar with an electric mixer at low speed, until light and fluffy. With the mixer running, add the eggs, one at a time, frequently scraping down the sides of the bowl. Add the sour cream, vanilla, and rum, and mix well.

Mix in some of the mashed plantains, then some of the flour mixture, repeating this until all of the plantain and flour mixture is incorporated.

Preheat the oven to 350°.

Divide the mixture equally between 2 buttered and floured 9-inch loaf pans. Bake until a toothpick comes out clean when inserted, 40 to 50 minutes.

YIELD: 2 LOAVES

Coconut Biscuits

This is a straightforward recipe that I first created to accompany the spicy shrimp stew, Enchilado de Camarones (page 114). These biscuits can also be served with spicy breakfast sausage.

2 cups all-purpose flour

1 tablespoon baking powder

¹/₂ teaspoon baking soda

¹/₂ teaspoon salt

5 tablespoons butter, at room temperature

³/₄ cup coconut milk

1 cup grated sweet coconut, toasted (page 7)

2 tablespoons melted butter

Sift the flour, baking powder, baking soda, and salt into a large mixing bowl. Add the butter and incorporate.

Add the coconut milk and grated coconut, reserving a bit of the coconut for the topping. Stir until the dough just holds together, about 1 minute.

Turn out the dough onto a lightly floured work surface and sprinkle with some flour. Knead for about 30 seconds.

Preheat the oven to 450°.

Roll out the dough to a thickness of about ³/₄ inch, then cut out the biscuits into 2-inch rounds.

Brush lightly with the melted butter and arrange on a greased baking sheet. Bake until lightly golden brown, 12 to 15 minutes.

Remove the biscuits from the oven and turn out onto wire racks to cool.

YIELD: 1 DOZEN BISCUITS

Anise Bread

This bread makes terrific sandwiches—cheese sandwiches in particular. It has an unexpected licorice flavor for a bread, especially if you're not anticipating the distinctive flavor of anise.

1 package active dry yeast
2 cups lukewarm water
1 tablespoon sugar
1 tablespoon salt
$\frac{1}{2}$ cup melted vegetable shortening
6 cups plus $\frac{1}{2}$ cup sifted bread flour
2 tablespoons milk
1 tablespoon anise seeds

In a mixing bowl sprinkle the yeast over the warm water and add 1 teaspoon of the sugar. Let proof for 5 to 10 minutes.

Stir in the remaining sugar, salt, and shortening. With an electric mixer, mix in the 6 cups of flour, 1 cup at a time, until a stiff dough forms.

Form the dough into a large ball and place in a lightly oiled bowl, turning to cover all sides. Cover the bowl with plastic wrap and let the dough rise in a warm place until doubled in volume, about 1$\frac{1}{2}$ hours.

Preheat the oven to 400°.

Turn out the dough onto a lightly floured work surface and knead for about 5 minutes, adding extra flour as necessary.

Shape into 2 long loaves, and place on a lightly buttered baking sheet. Make several slashes across the top of the loaves with a sharp knife. Brush each loaf lightly with the milk and sprinkle with the anise seeds. Let the loaves rest for 5 to 10 minutes.

Place a pan of water on the bottom of the oven (this will make the bread extra crusty while baking). Bake the loaves until crusty, 35 to 40 minutes.

Remove the bread from the oven and turn out onto wire racks to cool.

YIELD: 2 LOAVES

Coca a la Mallorqueña

This is the Spanish version of pizza. Coca means "open face," and Mallorqueña refers to the fact that this recipe is originally from the (Spanish) Mediterranean island of Majorca. There are various options for toppings, but the most important factor is to use only the finest ingredients. This is especially true for the olives—my preference is for the flavorful alphonso, niçoise, or black kalamatas—and anchovies.

1 tablespoon active dry yeast
1$\frac{1}{2}$ cups lukewarm water
2 tablespoons olive oil
1$\frac{1}{2}$ teaspoons salt
4 cups all-purpose flour
$\frac{1}{4}$ cup cornmeal

Suggested Toppings

$\frac{1}{4}$ cup caramelized onions
$\frac{1}{4}$ cup chopped pitted black olives
$\frac{1}{4}$ cup chopped sundried tomatoes
$\frac{1}{4}$ cup chopped anchovies

In the bowl of a food processor, sprinkle the yeast over the warm water. Let proof for 5 to 10 minutes.

Add the olive oil, salt, and 1 cup of the flour, and pulse for 1 minute. Add the remaining flour and pulse until a ball forms. (The dough will be sticky.)

Turn out the dough into a well-oiled bowl, turning the dough so that all sides of it are covered with the oil. Cover with plastic wrap and let the dough rise in a warm place until doubled in volume, 1 to 2 hours.

Preheat the oven to 450°.

Divide the dough into quarters and roll each portion into an oval shape. Place the ovals on a baking sheet that has been sprinkled with the cornmeal. Add your desired toppings and bake until golden brown, about 20 minutes.

YIELD: 8 SERVINGS

Olive Rolls

These are ideal rolls to accompany salads, which is the reason I created them in the first place. Bear in mind that their strong flavor can dominate other foods. They are wonderful just with a little olive oil or cream cheese. Use only the best-quality olives, such as the Greek kalamatas. You can substitute green olives, but I prefer the flavor and striking visual effect of the black.

1 teaspoon active dry yeast

2 cups lukewarm water

2 cups bread flour

1$\frac{1}{2}$ cups coarsely chopped kalamata olives

2 tablespoons olive oil

2 teaspoons salt

$\frac{1}{2}$ cup oat flour

3 cups whole-wheat flour

In a mixing bowl, sprinkle the yeast over the warm water. Let proof for 5 to 10 minutes.

Stirring constantly, add the bread flour gradually, then stir for an additional 3 minutes. Cover the bowl with plastic wrap and let sit until foamy, 30 to 40 minutes.

In a small bowl, combine the olives, olive oil, and salt, and stir into the yeast and flour mixture.

Stir in the oat flour, then stir in a cup at a time of the whole-wheat flour to form a soft dough. (You may need slightly more than 3 cups.)

Turn out the dough onto a lightly floured work surface and knead until elastic, about 8 minutes, adding more bread flour if sticky.

Place the dough in an oiled bowl, turning the dough so that all sides of it are covered with oil. Cover with plastic wrap and let the dough rise in a warm place until doubled in volume, about 2 hours.

Punch down the dough, divide it in half, and form 12 rolls out of each half. Place the rolls on a greased baking sheet, cover, and let rise again for about 40 minutes.

Preheat the oven to 425°.

Bake the rolls until golden brown, about 35 minutes. Remove the bread from the oven and turn out onto wire racks to cool.

YIELD: 2 DOZEN ROLLS

Medianoche Bread

I use this excellent egg bread recipe for my Medianoche Sandwich (page 62) and the Seafood Frita (page 61). If you're short on time, use the fast-rising yeast—a suggestion that applies to all the yeast breads in this chapter.

2 packages active dry yeast

2 cups lukewarm water

4 egg yolks, lightly beaten

3 tablespoons vegetable oil

$\frac{1}{4}$ cup sugar

1 tablespoon salt

6 cups all-purpose flour

Egg Wash

1 egg

1 tablespoon milk

In a mixing bowl, sprinkle the yeast over $\frac{1}{2}$ cup of the warm water. Let proof for 10 to 12 minutes.

Stir in the remaining water, egg yolks, oil, and sugar.

Sift the salt and flour into a mixing bowl. With an electric mixer, mix 5 cups of the flour mixture into the liquid ingredients, about $\frac{2}{3}$ cup at a time, until a dough forms.

Transfer to a lightly floured work surface and knead the dough for about 10 minutes, gradually adding the remaining flour. When soft and smooth, form into a large ball.

Place the dough in a well-oiled bowl, turning the dough so that all sides of it are covered with oil. Cover the bowl with plastic wrap and let the dough rise in a warm place until doubled in volume, 1 to 1$\frac{1}{2}$ hours.

Punch down the dough and return it to a lightly floured work surface. Knead briefly, then roll the dough into a ball. Cover with a damp towel and let the dough rest for 10 minutes.

Form the dough into 8 round or oblong rolls. Place on a cookie sheet lined with parchment paper, cover with a damp towel, and let rise again for 45 minutes.

Preheat the oven to 400°.

Beat the egg and milk together in a bowl and brush the rolls with the egg wash. Make a slash in the top of each roll with a sharp knife.

Bake the rolls until golden brown, 25 to 30 minutes. Remove from the oven and turn out onto wire racks to cool.

YIELD: 8 ROLLS

SALSAS & MOJOS

Opposite page: Anchovy Salsa (top left), Roasted Corn and Pepper Salsa (right), and Cachucha, Scotch Bonnet, and Green Tomato Salsa (bottom left)

ALSAS AND MOJOS are an important
element of Nuevo Latino cooking, and I serve
them with more than half of my dishes at
the restaurants. Salsas have become big news in
kitchens all across North America over the last
few years, to such an extent that they have now
replaced ketchup as the best-selling condiment.
Their close cousin, mojos, are spicy salsas of Spanish origin that typically contain garlic, citrus juice,
olive oil, and some type of herb. Mojos are more
liquid in consistency than salsas, and they're invariably served with cooked foods, which is not neces-
sarily true of salsas. My mother usually made her
mojo with sour orange juice and parsley and served
it with steak, pork, or roasted chicken.

Salsas and mojos are wonderful, healthful alternatives to sauces made with cream or butter. They
can provide a wide range and complexity of flavors but without the calories and cholesterol of
the richer sauces. Another advantage of salsas and
mojos is that they involve little or no cooking,

and you don't need to be a four-star chef to make
them. The combination of ingredients you can
use for them is virtually unlimited, and some of
the best salsas are made with commonly available
produce from the local market. And one thing's
for sure: the fresher, more colorful, and flavorful
the ingredients, the better these salsas are.

I first got turned on to making salsas by my
friend Carlitos, a food runner at Yuca in Miami
(you'll find his signature salsa recipe on page
40). He regularly made salsas for our staff meals
at the restaurant, and they were so good, I asked
him to make a different salsa for our main
course "special" each evening. I served my salsa
and mojo apprenticeship with Carlitos, and now
I make them like he did, instinctively, without
having to think about it. The more you make
them, the more you'll feel that way too.

All of these recipes should be used in 2 to
3 days because the citrus and other fruit juices
quickly lose their fresh flavor.

Cachucha, Scotch Bonnet, and Green Tomato Salsa

This spicy salsa is ideal with grouper or a grilled, moist fish like mackerel, sea bass, or kingfish. It also works well sprinkled over hearty soups or chunky stews, and it's just the thing for a summer backyard barbecue when you can pick fresh green tomatoes right off the vine. Pictured (bottom left) on page 36.

25 cachucha peppers, seeded and minced

2 Scotch bonnet chiles, seeded and minced

3 green tomatoes, cut into $^1/_2$-inch dice

1 red onion, cut into $^1/_2$-inch dice

3 tablespoons chopped chives

3 tablespoons chopped fresh cilantro leaves

$^1/_3$ cup freshly squeezed tangerine or orange juice

2 tablespoons extra virgin olive oil

Salt and pepper to taste

Combine all of the ingredients in a mixing bowl. Refrigerate for 3 to 4 hours before serving so that the flavors can marry. Keep refrigerated for up to 24 hours.

YIELD: APPROXIMATELY 3 CUPS

Roasted Corn and Pepper Salsa

This summertime salsa puts fresh corn to good use. The key to this recipe is blanching the corn before roasting it, which brings out its full sweetness. Blanching also preserves the corn, helping it last a little longer. I like to serve this tasty salsa with poultry dishes such as grilled chicken breasts or sautéed turkey breast, and with steaks or other cuts of beef. Pictured (right) on page 36.

1 canned chipotle chile, seeded and minced

1 ear fresh corn

1 red bell pepper, roasted, peeled, seeded, and cut into $^1/_2$-inch dice (page 6)

1 yellow bell pepper, roasted, peeled, seeded, and cut into $^1/_2$-inch dice (page 6)

1 green bell pepper, roasted, peeled, seeded, and cut into $^1/_2$-inch dice (page 6)

$^1/_2$ tablespoon chopped fresh oregano leaves

1 tomato, seeded and cut into $^1/_2$-inch dice

$^3/_4$ teaspoon sugar

$^1/_4$ cup olive oil

1$^1/_2$ tablespoons cider vinegar

Salt and pepper to taste

Blanch the corn for 1 minute, then roast (see page 6). Combine all of the ingredients in a mixing bowl. Refrigerate for up to 2 days.

YIELD: APPROXIMATELY 2 CUPS

Smoked Queso Blanco Salsa

Using cheese in a salsa may seem somewhat unusual, but this is a terrific dipping salsa for chips—especially plantain or yuca chips. You can use a different smoked cheese (such as Muenster) if the slightly salty queso blanco is unavailable. This salsa is best prepared at the last minute.

1 cucumber, washed

2 large tomatoes, cut into $^1/_4$-inch dice

1 red onion, cut into $^1/_4$-inch dice

2 tablespoons minced cilantro leaves

2 small jalapeño chiles, seeded and minced

Juice of 4 limes

$^1/_2$ cup olive oil

8 ounces smoked queso blanco, cut into $^1/_4$-inch dice

Salt and pepper to taste

Peel the cucumber, leaving a small amount of the flesh attached to the skin. Finely dice the peel and transfer to a mixing bowl, reserving the rest of the cucumber for another use.

Add the remaining ingredients to the bowl and thoroughly combine. Refrigerate for several hours before serving so that the flavors can marry. Serve the same day.

YIELD: APPROXIMATELY 3 CUPS

Cucumber-Dill Salsa

I created this salsa for smoked salmon or cooked salmon dishes. It's simple and easy to make, and it works best if you put the recipe together about an hour before you need it.

2 hothouse (seedless) cucumbers, unpeeled, and cut into $1/2$-inch dice
1 red onion, cut into $1/4$-inch dice
Juice of 2 lemons
2 tablespoons minced fresh dill
Salt to taste

Combine the cucumbers, onion, lemon juice, dill, and salt in a mixing bowl. Refrigerate until serving.

YIELD: APPROXIMATELY 2 CUPS

Pickled Onion and Pepper Salsa

This vinegary salsa is wonderful with crispy fried fish or even fried mushrooms. When I was growing up, we always had a jar of it on hand.

2 small red onions, cut into $1/4$-inch dice
20 to 30 cachucha peppers, halved and seeded
1 cup white wine vinegar
2 teaspoons salt
1 tablespoon sugar

Place the onions and peppers in a large, glass bottling jar. Combine the vinegar, salt, and sugar and pour over the onions and peppers. Seal tightly and let sit for 2 to 3 days at room temperature.

YIELD: APPROXIMATELY 2 CUPS

Dried Shrimp Salsa

This assertive, textured salsa goes very well with grilled or steamed fish dishes. At the restaurant, we serve it with the Sugarcane Tuna (page 104). In fact, its robust flavor complements any mild fish. The dried shrimp is available in Asian markets.

1 large cucumber, washed
6 ounces unsalted peanuts
2 large tomatoes, seeded and cut into $1/2$-inch dice
1 red bell pepper, seeded and cut into $1/2$-inch dice
2 jalapeño chiles, seeded and minced
1 red onion, cut into $1/2$-inch dice
3 tablespoons chopped chives
3 tablespoons chopped cilantro
Juice of 4 limes
Juice of 2 lemons
$2/3$ cup olive oil
6 ounces dried tiny shrimp
Salt and pepper to taste

Peel the cucumber, leaving a small amount of the flesh attached to the peel. Finely dice the peel and transfer to a mixing bowl, reserving the rest of the cucumber for another use.

Add the peanuts, tomatoes, bell pepper, jalapeños, onion, chives, cilantro, citrus juices, olive oil, and shrimp to the bowl and toss well. Season with salt and pepper. (If making the salsa ahead of time, keep refrigerated and mix in the shrimp just before serving so they stay crunchy.)

YIELD: APPROXIMATELY 3 CUPS

Salsita de Carlitos

This salsa is named after one of my best buddies, Carlos Sorida, who has always been like a brother to me. We cooked and ate together, and we shared many similar interests. Carlos comes from Guadalajara in Mexico and this is his recipe. I use it all the time, and it's also the base for many of my other salsas. Serve it with chips, as a garnish for fish, and as an all-round, multipurpose salsa. This salsa is best when served the same day.

2 cucumbers, washed
3 large tomatoes, seeded and cut into $1/2$-inch dice
3 jalapeño chiles, seeded and minced
$1/4$ cup minced fresh cilantro leaves
1 large red onion, diced
Juice of 2 lemons
$1/4$ cup red wine vinegar
$2/3$ cup olive oil
Salt and pepper to taste

Peel the cucumbers, leaving a small amount of the flesh attached to the peel. Finely dice the peel and transfer to a mixing bowl, reserving the rest of the cucumber for another use.

Add the remaining ingredients to the bowl, and mix well.

YIELD: APPROXIMATELY 4 CUPS

Anchovy Salsa

This is another recipe inspired by my wife, who made me a wonderful dish with little anchovies and roasted bell pepper strips. I like to eat this salsa with plain croutons or chips. Pictured (top left) on page 36.

1 large green bell pepper, roasted, peeled, seeded, and cut into $^1/_2$-inch dice (page 6)
1 large yellow bell pepper, roasted, peeled, seeded, and cut into $^1/_2$-inch dice (page 6)
1 small red onion, cut into $^1/_2$-inch dice
3 cloves garlic, minced
3 tablespoons chopped fresh parsley
2 small cans (2 ounces each) anchovies, drained, patted dry, and chopped
Juice of 2 lemons
$^1/_2$ cup olive oil
Pepper to taste

Combine all of the ingredients in a mixing bowl. Keep refrigerated for up to 24 hours.

YIELD: APPROXIMATELY 2 CUPS

Roasted Pear, Onion, and Walnut Salsa

Try this salsa on top of a mesclun (mixed) salad, on its own, or topped with some crumbled goat cheese. It's a great alternative to salad dressing, and the ingredients provide crunch and texture—absolutely wonderful. Use it as a mild, sweet accompaniment to sliced, cold meat, or with assertive meats like lamb and venison.

1 large white onion, quartered
3 Bartlett pears, peeled, halved, cored, and seeded
$^1/_2$ teaspoon ground cinnamon
$^1/_2$ teaspoon ground allspice
1 tablespoon honey
Juice of 3 lemons
1 tablespoon finely chopped chives
$^1/_2$ cup chopped walnuts
$^1/_4$ cup toasted walnut oil

Preheat the oven to 400°.

Place the onion quarters and pears on a baking sheet and bake in the oven until the edges are browned, about 20 minutes. Remove from the oven and let cool for about 1 hour.

Dice the onion and pears and transfer to a mixing bowl. Add the remaining ingredients and thoroughly combine. Refrigerate for 1 hour and serve.

YIELD: APPROXIMATELY 3 CUPS

Dried Mango–Toasted Coconut Salsa

The different textures in this tropical salsa make it fun to eat. It goes well with grilled shrimp and most spicy foods. Dried mango can be found in Asian markets and some health food stores.

$^1/_3$ cup coconut milk
2 tablespoons grated gingerroot
2 tablespoons freshly squeezed lime juice
1 tablespoon sugar
1 pound dried mango, cut into $^1/_4$-inch dice
3 jalapeño chiles, seeded and minced
$^1/_2$ cup seeded and diced red bell pepper
$^1/_2$ cup diced red onion
3 tablespoons minced cilantro leaves
3 ounces dried unsweetened coconut, toasted (page 7)

Place the coconut milk, ginger, lime juice, and sugar in a blender and blend well on high speed.

Place the mango, jalapeños, bell pepper, onion, and cilantro in a mixing bowl. Pour in the blended coconut milk mixture and thoroughly combine. Stir in the toasted coconut just before serving.

YIELD: APPROXIMATELY 2 CUPS

Plantain, Pineapple, and Serrano Salsa

What I like most about this salsa is the combination of sweetness from the pineapple and plantain and spiciness from the serranos and mustard. It also contains different textures, some chewy and some crisp. This is an ideal salsa for sautéed salmon, and really, just about anything grilled. To add a tropical touch when serving this salsa, garnish the plates with some of the leaves from the crown of the pineapple and some fresh pineapple slices.

$^1/_2$ cup vegetable oil

1 large semiripe plantain, peeled and cut into $^1/_2$-inch dice

1 small red onion, cut into $^1/_2$-inch dice

$^1/_2$ cup seeded and diced red bell pepper

$^1/_2$ cup seeded and minced serrano chiles

$^1/_4$ cup mustard seeds

2 tablespoons finely chopped scallions

2 tablespoons finely chopped chives

$^3/_4$ cup diced fresh pineapple

$^1/_4$ cup fresh pineapple juice

1 tablespoon Dijon mustard

Salt and pepper to taste

Heat the oil in a sauté pan and fry the plantain until golden brown. Drain on paper towels and transfer to a mixing bowl. Add the remaining ingredients to the bowl and thoroughly combine. Keep refrigerated. (Best used the same day.)

YIELD: APPROXIMATELY 3 CUPS

Papaya-Mustard Salsa

Papayas are usually shipped and sold under-ripe, and that's how you want them for this recipe: firm, and somewhere between greenish-ripe and fully ripe. The mild flavor of papaya in this salsa is best brought out when paired with a non-oily fish such as snapper, grouper, or mahimahi. It also goes with meats, and I use this salsa with my Pulled Pork and Gouda Baguette (page 64).

2 teaspoons mustard seeds

1 teaspoon Dijon mustard

Juice of 4 limes

Juice of 1 orange

2 tablespoons olive oil

1 firm papaya, peeled, seeded, and cut into $^1/_2$-inch dice

$^1/_2$ red onion, cut into $^1/_4$-inch dice

$^1/_2$ red bell pepper, seeded and cut into $^1/_2$-inch dice

3 jalapeño chiles, roasted, seeded, and minced (page 6)

2 scallions, minced

1 teaspoon chopped fresh cilantro leaves

Salt and pepper to taste

In a mixing bowl, combine the mustard seeds, mustard, and citrus juices. Whisk in the olive oil in a slow, steady stream.

Combine the remaining ingredients in a separate bowl, and fold in the mustard mixture. Refrigerate for 2 to 3 hours before serving so that the flavors can marry. Use the same day.

YIELD: APPROXIMATELY 3 CUPS

Banana-Lime Salsa

This is a tasty accompaniment for grilled chicken or duck breast. Because the bananas will quickly ripen and become mushy, the salsa has a very limited shelf life and is best served as soon as you've made it.

3 firm semiripe bananas, peeled and finely diced

Juice of 1 lime

3 limes, peeled and sectioned

1 teaspoon honey

2 jalapeño chiles, seeded and minced

Place the bananas in a mixing bowl and sprinkle with the lime juice. Toss gently and thoroughly so that the bananas don't turn brown.

Add the lime sections, honey, and jalapeños, and toss well. Serve immediately.

YIELD: APPROXIMATELY 2 CUPS

Lychee, Ginger, and Banana Salsa

There is only a short season for fresh lychees, but when they're available this is the salsa to make. In the summer, I buy several pounds of lychees at a time, keep them refrigerated, and eat them while I can. I developed this recipe at home, at the end of the lychee season, when I wanted to use them up. I made it for some stone crabs, and it proved to be terrific. It also goes particularly well with duck breast.

1 pound fresh lychees, peeled and seeded

2 tablespoons minced gingerroot

2 semiripe bananas, peeled and diced

3 tablespoons freshly squeezed lime juice

Combine the lychees, ginger, bananas, and juice in a mixing bowl. Toss well, and serve immediately.

YIELD: APPROXIMATELY 3 CUPS

Ruby Grapefruit, Shallot, and Cilantro Mojo

This mojo is excellent with steamed, cold shrimp or lobster, or just about any cold seafood. It makes a great dipping sauce for stone crabs, and it can also be used as a salad dressing—so if you have some cold seafood left over, add it to a salad and toss with this mojo.

3/4 cup olive oil
3 shallots, finely sliced
2 ruby grapefruits, peeled
    and sectioned
3 tablespoons chopped fresh cilantro leaves
Salt to taste

    Heat the olive oil in a sauté pan or skillet and sauté the shallots over low heat until tender, about 5 minutes.

    Cut the grapefruit sections in half and add to the pan for the final minute or so. Transfer to a bowl and let the mixture cool completely. Mix in the cilantro and season with salt. Keep refrigerated for up to 2 days.

YIELD: APPROXIMATELY 3 CUPS

Sour Orange, Red Onion, and Parsley Mojo

This recipe differs slightly from classic mojo in that it uses red onion instead of garlic. It's best to make this mojo a bit ahead of time so that the color of the red onion "bleeds" into the sour orange. The traditional accompaniment is grilled pork, but it's also wonderful with well-roasted chicken—charring its skin brings out the full flavors of the mojo. Pictured (top) on page 45.

Juice of 5 Seville (sour) oranges
    (about 1 cup)
1 red onion, cut into 1/4-inch dice
1/4 cup chopped flat-leaf parsley
1/2 cup olive oil
1 teaspoon salt

    Place the orange juice, onion, parsley, olive oil, and salt in a mixing bowl and blend well using a wire whisk. Keep refrigerated for up to 2 days.

YIELD: APPROXIMATELY 2 CUPS

Lime, Garlic, and Oregano Mojo

This is the "he-man" of mojos, and the classic combination of lime, garlic, and oregano is a must for grilled red meats. Try it with flank steaks, T-bones, sirloin steaks, or lamb.

3/4 cup olive oil
1 1/2 cups freshly squeezed lime juice
3 tablespoons minced garlic
1 teaspoon ground cumin
1/2 cup chopped fresh oregano leaves
1 1/2 teaspoons salt

    With a wire whisk, blend the olive oil, lime juice, garlic, cumin, oregano, and salt in a mixing bowl. Keep refrigerated for up to 2 days.

YIELD: APPROXIMATELY 2 1/2 CUPS

Mango-Mint Mojo

This is a mojo I created by accident when we had a lot of mangoes on hand. On that occasion, we served it as a dressing for some cold calamari, but it also works well with any cold seafood, fried fish, or sautéed veal. This may not be a traditional mojo in that I've omitted the oil, but the sweetness of the mango and the freshness of the mint make a great combination. Pictured (bottom) on page 45.

2 ripe mangoes, peeled, pitted,
    and chopped
1/2 cup freshly squeezed lime juice
1/2 cup chopped fresh mint leaves

    Place the mango, lime juice, and mint in a blender, and purée. Keep refrigerated for up to 2 days.

YIELD: APPROXIMATELY 2 CUPS

Lemon, Thyme, and Chive Mojo

If you make this mojo ahead of time, add the chives at the last minute, or else the lemon juice will dull their vivid color. Try this mojo with roasted meats, especially poultry, or oily fish such as mackerel or kingfish. My mother used to make a fantastic version of this mojo at Thanksgiving; its flavors go particularly well with turkey and cranberry sauce.

3 tablespoons minced thyme
1/2 cup finely chopped chives
2 tablespoons minced garlic
1 cup freshly squeezed lemon juice
1/4 cup extra virgin olive oil
Salt and pepper to taste

Combine the thyme, chives, garlic, lemon juice, olive oil, and salt and pepper in a mixing bowl and serve immediately.

YIELD: APPROXIMATELY 2 CUPS

Mojo Light

Here's another mojo that breaks with tradition. I created it for some of our restaurant guests who wanted the flavor of the mojo without any of the fat content. This is a herb mojo that's simple to make and perfect for anyone on a diet. (You should serve it as soon as you've puréed it or the lemon juice will leach the bright chlorophyll color of the herbs.) It's wonderful with firm, meaty fish like tuna or swordfish.

2 tablespoons chopped flat-leaf parsley
2 tablespoons chopped fresh parsley
2 tablespoons chopped fresh oregano leaves
2 tablespoons chopped garlic
1 cup freshly squeezed lime juice
1 teaspoon salt

Place the parsleys, oregano, garlic, lime juice, and salt in a blender and purée. Serve immediately.

YIELD: APPROXIMATELY 1 1/4 CUPS

Spicy Sage and Garlic-Pineapple Mojo

Here's another twist on the classic mojo. Try it at Thanksgiving. It makes an excellent accompaniment for turkey, and a great alternative to cranberry sauce on cold turkey sandwiches.

1/2 cup olive oil
2 tablespoons minced garlic
1/2 cup puréed ripe pineapple
3 tablespoons chopped fresh sage leaves
2 tablespoons chopped fresh parsley
1 teaspoon crushed red pepper flakes
Salt and pepper to taste

Heat the olive oil in a small skillet and sauté the garlic over medium heat for 2 minutes. Add the pineapple, cook for another 2 minutes, and transfer to a mixing bowl. Add the sage, parsley, red pepper, and salt and pepper, and mix well. Let cool for 15 minutes before serving.

YIELD: APPROXIMATELY 1 CUP

Papaya, Rosemary, and Garlic Mojo

One afternoon, I went fishing in Biscayne Bay and caught a large snapper. A couple of hours later, I roasted it and made up this mojo to go with it. It was so outstanding that I added it to my restaurant repertoire. It goes very well with any firm-fleshed fish, and even lamb. Pictured (left) on opposite page.

2 tablespoons olive oil
1 tablespoon minced garlic
1 ripe papaya, peeled, seeded, and cut into 1/2-inch dice
1 tablespoon chopped fresh rosemary leaves
1 teaspoon sugar
Salt and pepper to taste

Heat the olive oil in a pan or skillet and sauté the garlic over medium heat for 3 minutes. Add the papaya, rosemary, sugar, and salt and pepper and remove from the heat. Let cool, transfer to a mixing bowl, and chill in the refrigerator before serving.

YIELD: 1 TO 1 1/2 CUPS

Oppostie page: Sour Orange, Red Onion, and Parsley Mojo (top); Mango-Mint Mojo (bottom); and Papaya, Rosemary, and Garlic Mojo (left)

SALADS & SANDWICHES

Oppostie page: Three-Bean Salad with Grilled Scallops

LATIN AMERICAN SALADS tend to be based not on leafy greens but on vegetables and other ingredients that are cooked, chilled, and mixed together. Many of the recipes in this chapter follow that style. However, things are changing, and fresh green salads are becoming increasingly popular, perhaps because of the influence of North American and European cuisines.

In Cuba, a salad often means watercress—my father eats it all the time. I rarely ate a salad when I was growing up, and like many American kids of my generation, it was iceberg lettuce with tomatoes when I did eat one. Now that so many interesting greens have reached the market, it's more exciting and a lot easier to make great salads.

At my restaurants, we routinely offer a mixed green salad as a side dish for the main course, and I also use many of the recipes that follow. I believe in putting a lot of thought into dressings, because they are one of the most important flavor components of a salad. And I like to draw on the cuisines of different countries in creating my recipes for salads and dressings.

If Latin Americans underachieve in their consumption of salads, they make up for it in their enthusiasm for sandwiches. As the saying goes, "If you can't put it between two slices of bread, it's not worth eating." At the restaurants, we always have a sandwich on the menu, and sometimes we also feature one as a special of the day. For the serious sandwich connoisseur, I highly recommend investing in a sandwich press for toasting the bread and giving the sandwich a crisp and delicious texture.

Banana-Lentil Salad

This classic salad originates in the Spanish Canary Islands, where it is traditionally enjoyed as an accompaniment for rabbit. It's also perfect with fried oysters or roasted salmon. The pairing of bananas and lentils may sound highly unusual, but the flavors work very well together. The salad will keep for 2 to 3 days in the refrigerator.

1 cup brown lentils

1 cup yellow or red lentils

3 tablespoons olive oil

1 red onion, cut into $^1/_4$-inch dice

1 red bell pepper, cut into $^1/_4$-inch dice

1 tablespoon finely minced garlic

2 tablespoons chopped parsley

3 tablespoons chopped cilantro leaves

3 semiripe bananas, peeled and chopped

$^1/_4$ cup balsamic vinegar

Salt and pepper to taste

Place the lentils in a large bowl, cover with plenty of water, and soak overnight.

The next day, drain off the water, rinse the lentils, and transfer to a saucepan. Add fresh water to cover by at least an inch.

Bring the lentils to a boil. Lower the heat and simmer for 6 minutes. Remove the pan from the heat, drain, and transfer to a mixing bowl to cool.

In a sauté pan or skillet, heat the olive oil. Add the onion, bell pepper, and garlic and sauté over medium heat until tender, about 2 minutes.

Add the onion mixture to the cooled lentils and stir in the remaining ingredients. Mix thoroughly.

Let the salad chill for 1 to 2 hours before serving.

YIELD: 8 TO 10 SERVINGS

Avocado Salad

This version of avocado salad is not to be confused with guacamole. The success of this recipe depends on using perfectly ripe avocados—if they're overripe or underripe, the full flavors and proper texture just won't emerge. This salad is best served as soon as you've made it, and you should try to use it up the same day. I especially like to use this salad as a side dish for sandwiches.

3 ripe but firm Haas avocados, pitted and peeled

$^1/_4$ cup finely chopped scallions

1 large red bell pepper, seeded and cut into $^1/_2$-inch dice

1 red onion, cut into $^1/_2$-inch dice

$^1/_4$ cup chopped cilantro leaves

1 cucumber, peeled, seeded, halved lengthwise and cut into half-moons

1 small tomato, seeded and finely chopped

$^1/_4$ cup freshly squeezed lime juice

2 tablespoons extra virgin olive oil

Salt and pepper to taste

Cut the avocados into bite-sized chunks and place in a large bowl. Add the scallions, bell pepper, onion, cilantro, cucumber, tomato, and lime juice, and toss gently.

Add the olive oil and the salt and pepper. Gently stir and serve.

YIELD: 4 SERVINGS

Ensalada Bacalao
with Red Peppers and Avocado

I could eat bacalao (dried salt cod) seven days a week. Drying and salting cod was the preferred means of preserving it in the days before refrigeration, and it's one of my all-time favorite foods. (I think I could write a bacalao cookbook with 365 recipes, one for every day of the year!) It can take some time to acquire a taste for bacalao, but it's worth it. I prefer this dish hot, but it can also be served cold.

1 pound bacalao

1 tablespoon olive oil

$^{1}/_{2}$ cup diced white onion

3 cloves garlic, minced

$^{1}/_{2}$ cup diced tomato

Juice of 2 lemons

2 tablespoons chopped parsley

Pepper to taste

1 tablespoon mayonnaise

Vinaigrette

$^{1}/_{4}$ cup aged sherry vinegar

1 teaspoon Colman's dry mustard

1 teaspoon minced garlic

$^{1}/_{2}$ cup olive oil

3 red bell peppers, roasted, peeled, seeded, and sliced (page 6)

3 ripe avocados, halved, pitted, peeled, and sliced

Soak the bacalao overnight in a large pan of water.

Drain the water from the bacalao and add fresh water to the pan. Bring to a boil, then lower the heat and cook over medium-high heat for 30 minutes.

Drain off the water and replace with fresh water. Bring to a boil, then lower the heat and simmer for another 30 minutes. Repeat, simmering for another 30 minutes. (*Note:* This process of draining and replacing water is necessary in order to remove salt.) Drain the water for the final time, flake the cooked fish with a fork, and set aside to cool.

Heat the olive oil in a skillet. Add the onion and garlic and sauté over high heat for 2 minutes. Add the tomatoes, flaked bacalao, and lemon juice, stir, and cook for 1 minute.

Remove the pan from the heat and let cool slightly. Add the parsley, pepper, and mayonnaise and stir well. Chill in the refrigerator until ready to serve.

To prepare the vinaigrette, whisk the vinegar, mustard, and garlic together in a bowl. While whisking rapidly, add the olive oil in a slow, steady stream until emulsified.

To serve, assemble in layers. Place one eighth of the bacalao mixture in the center of each serving plate, and smooth out to form an even layer. Place a roasted bell pepper slice on top of this, followed by an avocado slice. Repeat for 3 layers, stacking each in the same way. Sprinkle the salad and plate with the vinaigrette.

YIELD: 4 SERVINGS

Opposite page: Ensalada Bacalao with Red Peppers and Avocado

Peruvian Causa

Every time I've eaten causa, a layered, chilled potato salad, it's been completely different. The very first time I tried it, at a Peruvian restaurant in Miami, it was made with layers of mashed white potatoes, chopped olives, and tomatoes between the layers. The next time, prepared at the home of a Peruvian friend, it came molded in a cup, with crab-meat, a layer of yellow potato that had been cooked with saffron, and a layer of regular white potato. When I encountered it on my travels in Peru, it was made with blue potatoes and tuna salad. Apparently, the recipe changes from town to town.

If you can't find blue potatoes for this recipe, substitute one of the other varieties of potato. Causa should be made at least 1 day in advance to allow the flavors to permeate the potatoes. It can be made in individual cups, but my preference is to make it in a loaf pan, which allows you to make attractive slices, like a terrine.

2 yellow potatoes (16 ounces), peeled and
    cut into $1/2$-inch dice
2 blue potatoes (16 ounces), peeled and
    cut into $1/2$-inch dice
2 baking potatoes (16 ounces), peeled and
    cut into $1/2$-inch dice
Pinch saffron
$41/2$ tablespoons butter
Salt to taste

Olive Mixture

$1/3$ cup finely diced black olives
    (preferably niçoise, alphonso,
    or kalamata)
$1/3$ cup minced green olives
    (preferably manzilla or apercina)
3 cloves garlic, minced
2 tablespoons minced capers
2 tablespoons minced parsley
1 red bell pepper, roasted, peeled, seeded,
    and cut into $1/2$-inch dice (page 6)
1 tablespoon olive oil
Zest of 1 lemon, grated
Juice of 1 lemon

Place each variety of potato in a separate saucepan, adding the saffron to the yellow potato. Cover each with water and cook over medium heat until tender, 15 to 20 minutes.

Drain the water from the potatoes, then mash each separately with a potato masher or fork. Add $11/2$ tablespoons of the butter and the salt to each. Set aside.

In a mixing bowl, combine the olive mixture ingredients and set aside.

Grease a 9 by 4-inch loaf pan and line it with plastic wrap. (The wrap should extend over the edges of the pan by a couple of inches on all sides.) Layer one variety of mashed potatoes in the bottom of the pan and spread evenly. Spread half of the olive mixture on top of the potato layer and then add a layer of another variety of potato over the olive mixture. Add a final layer of the olive mixture, and finish with a layer of the remaining variety of potato. Fold the plastic wrap over to cover the top layer, and chill in the refrigerator for 2 to 3 hours.

Unfold the top covering of plastic wrap and gently invert the loaf pan onto a serving platter. Carefully remove the plastic wrap, and cut the causa into slices. If you like, you can serve it with the Huancaina Sauce (page 57) or the Anchovy Salsa (page 41).

YIELD: 8 SERVINGS

Opposite page: Peruvian Causa

Hearts of Palm and Orange Salad with Mâche

I wish fresh hearts of palm were generally available, because the difference in taste between fresh and canned hearts of palm is like that between fresh and canned asparagus. This recipe uses the canned variety, but if you can locate fresh ones, boil 1 pound for 4 minutes, cool, and proceed with the recipe. I was lucky enough to find a source for fresh hearts of palm about 3 years ago when I took a trip to Costa Rica to meet with a plantation owner who grew yuca. At that time we were going through at least 300 pounds of yuca a week (appropriately, because I was at Yuca restaurant in Miami). While I was in Costa Rica, my contact asked me to try some fresh hearts of palm, which I'd never seen before. I placed a standing order then and there for the restaurant.

Mâche, also known as corn salad or lamb's lettuce, is a tender, tangy field green that should be used as fresh as possible as it doesn't keep well. Pictured on page ii.

2 oranges, for garnish (optional)
1 small red onion, halved and julienned
8 ounces lump crabmeat, picked through
1 tablespoon chopped cilantro
1 tablespoon olive oil
2 cans (16 ounces each) hearts of palm, patted dry and sliced lengthwise

Cumin Vinaigrette

1 teaspoon toasted cumin seeds (page 7)
1 teaspoon grated orange zest
1 teaspoon chopped garlic
$1/4$ cup olive oil
$1/4$ cup sherry vinegar
Salt to taste

8 ounces mâche or Bibb lettuce
3 navel oranges, peeled and sectioned

Using an automatic citrus peeler, peel the 2 oranges. Cut zest into 4- to 5-inch-long pieces. Wrap each piece around a plastic straw. Place straws in a dehydrator or oven set at 200° overnight. Slide pieces off straws and reserve.

Place the onion, crabmeat, cilantro, and olive oil, in a mixing bowl and toss. Keep refrigerated until ready to serve.

Place the vinaigrette ingredients in a blender and blend for 5 seconds on high speed. Toss the mâche and orange sections in a mixing bowl.

To serve, stack 3 to 4 pieces of hearts of palm on individual plates. Spoon the crab mixture into the center of the stacks. Top each with the mâche and orange mixture. Drizzle with the vinaigrette. Garnish with the reserved orange zest spirals.

YIELD: 6 SERVINGS

Watercress and Tomato Salad with Peanut Dressing

In this recipe, Nuevo Latino meets Asia. Watercress is used extensively as a salad green in Cuba and some other Latin countries, and this is a simple and attractively peppery salad. Lighter than the Thai style of peanut dressing, it makes a wonderful dressing or dip for grilled chicken. It can be made ahead of time and kept in the refrigerator for 2 to 3 days.

Peanut Dressing

2 tablespoons smooth peanut butter
1 teaspoon chopped garlic
3 tablespoons chopped cilantro leaves
1 tablespoon chopped red bell pepper
1 jalapeño chile, seeded and chopped
2 tablespoons freshly squeezed lime juice
$1/4$ cup vegetable oil

Salad

3 beefsteak tomatoes, cut into 12 slices, $1/2$ to $3/4$ inch thick
1 small red onion, thinly sliced
4 cups watercress

Place all of the dressing ingredients in a blender and blend for 1 minute on high speed.

Arrange 3 tomato slices in a fan on each plate. Place the onion slices on top of the tomatoes and the watercress over the onions. Drizzle some dressing over each salad and serve.

YIELD: 4 SERVINGS

Three-Bean Salad with Grilled Scallops

Settle for nothing less than an incredibly fresh and tasty three-bean salad. The first time I made one, I was working at a hotel in Miami. I was due to make a three-bean salad for Sunday brunch, and I think the head chef was expecting me to open a can of garbanzos, a can of red kidney beans, defrost some green beans, and throw them together. Instead, I took dried black, red, and white beans—three varieties Latin cooks use most— and made everything from scratch. The result was a beautiful salad of vibrant color and flavor that looked like confetti. Was the chef surprised! Pictured on page 46.

Red Tomato Marinade (page 12)
32 large scallops (about 3 pounds)

4 ounces dried black beans
(about ³/₄ cup), soaked overnight
4 ounces dried red kidney beans
(about ³/₄ cup), soaked overnight
4 ounces dried Great Northern white
beans (about ³/₄ cup), soaked overnight

Dressing

1 small red onion, halved and thinly
sliced in half-moons
1 tablespoon chopped chives
1 teaspoon minced garlic
3 tablespoons diced red bell pepper
1 teaspoon chopped parsley
1 teaspoon chopped cilantro leaves
3 scallions, thinly sliced
Juice of 3 limes
¹/₄ cup olive oil
2 tablespoons balsamic vinegar
Salt and pepper to taste

Garnish

8 sprigs watercress
1 lime, cut into 8 wedges

Prepare the marinade in a large bowl. Add the scallops and let sit in the refrigerator for at least 6 hours.

Place each type of bean in a separate saucepan with their soaking water. Bring to a boil. Lower the heat, cover with lids, and simmer over medium heat for about 45 minutes, adding more water as necessary to keep the beans covered with water.

Remove the pans from the heat, keeping them covered. Let the beans cool in their cooking liquid for 1 to 2 hours. This will keep the beans tender and moist. Drain, pat dry, and mix the beans together in a large mixing bowl.

Combine all the dressing ingredients in a separate mixing bowl and mix well. Pour the dressing over the beans, toss, and refrigerate until ready to serve.

Prepare the grill. Grill the marinated scallops over medium heat for about 1 minute on each side. (As an alternative, you can pan-fry them.)

To serve, spoon the dressed bean salad onto the center of serving plates or into bowls, and place 4 grilled scallops per serving on top of the beans. Garnish with the watercress sprigs and lime wedges.

YIELD: 8 SERVINGS

Boniato and Shrimp Salad with Huancaina Sauce

The Huancayo Indians of Peru created this rich, classic sauce that is given its vibrant, yellow color by the eggs and turmeric. It's the perfect foil for the flavors of the tender, chilled boniato and shrimp, and it has also proved popular when I've served it with salmon roe caviar.

Huancaina Sauce

3 tablespoons vegetable oil
1 white onion, chopped
3 cloves garlic, chopped
2 hard-boiled eggs, sliced
1 tablespoon ground turmeric
1 can (10 ounces) evaporated milk
3 ounces feta cheese
3 ounces cream cheese
10 saltine crackers, crumbled
Salt to taste

Salad

2 large boniatos, peeled and
    cut into 1/2-inch dice
1 tablespoon salt
4 scallions (green and white parts), sliced
4 green or red jalapeño chiles, seeded and
    julienned
1 small red onion, halved and
    thinly sliced in half-moons
2 tablespoons olive oil
Salt and pepper to taste
1 bunch chives, tops cut into 4-inch
    lengths, for garnish

Shrimp Boil

30 to 40 large shrimp (about 2 pounds),
    peeled and deveined
1 cup white wine
2 tablespoons pickling spice
8 cloves garlic
1 teaspoon peppercorns
3 tablespoons Tabasco sauce
1 lemon, halved
3 tablespoons Worcestershire sauce
1 tablespoon angostura bitters
1 teaspoon chopped fresh thyme leaves
2 quarts water

To prepare the sauce, heat the oil in a sauté pan or skillet, add the onion, garlic, and eggs, and sauté over medium-low heat until the onions are translucent, about 5 minutes.

Stir in the turmeric and sauté for another 2 minutes. Stir in the evaporated milk and simmer for 3 minutes. Remove the pan from the heat and let the mixture cool briefly.

Transfer the mixture to a blender. Add the feta, cream cheese, and crackers, and blend on low speed until smooth. Add the salt and chill in the refrigerator.

To prepare the salad, place the boniato in a saucepan and cover with water. Add the salt and boil for 12 to 15 minutes, covered, over medium heat. Drain the boniato and place in a colander under cold running water until completely cool. Pat dry.

Transfer the boniato to a large mixing bowl; toss with the scallions, jalapeños, onion, and olive oil. Season with salt and pepper. Keep refrigerated until ready to serve.

Setting the shrimp aside, place the remaining ingredients in a large saucepan and bring to a boil. Reduce the heat and simmer for 10 minutes. Strain the liquid into a clean saucepan, discard the solids, and bring to a boil. Add the shrimp. Cook for $2^1/_2$ minutes, remove the shrimp, and immediately shock in a bowl of ice water.

To serve, spoon 3 tablespoons of the sauce onto each serving plate. Place the boniato salad in the center of the sauce and arrange the shrimp decoratively around the salad. Garnish with the chives.

YIELD: 6 SERVINGS

Opposite page: Boniato and Shrimp Salad with Huancaina Sauce

Grilled Flank Steak over Mushroom Ceviche

The first time I ever tried this Peruvian classic was when I visited my dad at work. He's a barber, and an enthusiastic Peruvian customer insisted that we try his recipe for mushroom ceviche. (You could tell he was enthusiastic because he brought his ceviche with him!) We loved it. It was just regular field mushrooms marinated in lemon and lime juice, and this recipe builds on that simple formula. The smaller the mushrooms the better, so if you can't find button mushrooms, cut the regular-sized ones into quarters.

13-pound flank steak
2 cups Fresh Cilantro Adobo (page 11)

Mushroom Ceviche

2 pounds button or tiny field mushrooms,
    washed and stems removed
1/3 cup freshly squeezed lemon juice
1/2 cup freshly squeezed lime juice
1/3 cup freshly squeezed orange juice
1/3 cup olive oil
1 small red onion, thinly sliced

1 small red bell pepper, seeded and
    julienned
3 cloves garlic, squeezed through
    a garlic press
1 tablespoon chopped cilantro leaves
Salt and pepper to taste

6 ounces mixed baby greens, washed
    and patted dry
12 triangle-shaped toast pieces,
    for garnish

Marinate the steak in the Fresh Cilantro Adobo for 12 hours.

Place the mushrooms in a mixing bowl. Add the citrus juices and olive oil, and toss. Let sit at room temperature for 1 hour, tossing occasionally.

Add the onion, bell pepper, garlic, cilantro, and salt and pepper, and mix well. Let sit in the refrigerator to marinate the mushrooms, about 2 hours.

Heat the grill to medium-high and grill the marinated flank steak for 7 minutes on each side for medium-rare. Slice thinly and serve over the Mushroom Ceviche with the mixed greens and toast triangles.

YIELD: 6 SERVINGS

Nicaraguan Vigoron Salad

If you've ever tasted the classic Nicaraguan salad called vigoron, you'll recognize the origin of this recipe. It contains a great variety of textures and flavors. It's important that the chicharrones (pork cracklings) are hot and that the cabbage is at room temperature. When I make this salad at home, I leave out the chicharrones to minimize cholesterol, but if you want to stick with tradition keep them in.

1 pound yuca, peeled, cored,
    cut lengthwise into wide strips, and
    placed in water
9 ounces white cabbage, thinly sliced
    like coleslaw
2 ripe tomatoes, cut into 1/2-inch dice
1 small red onion, halved and thinly sliced
    into half-moons
Juice of 5 limes
1 clove garlic, minced
3 tablespoons olive oil
Salt to taste

4 ounces chicharrones (optional)

Drain the yuca, add to a saucepan of salted water (use about 1/2 teaspoon salt) and bring to a boil. Reduce the heat and simmer until tender, about 25 minutes. Drain, pat dry, and set aside.

Preheat the oven to 400°.

Place the cabbage in a large mixing bowl and toss with the tomatoes, onion, lime juice, garlic, and olive oil. Season with salt and set aside.

Arrange the chicharrones in a single layer on a baking sheet and place in the oven until warm, 3 to 4 minutes.

To serve, place the cooked yuca on the bottom of a large serving platter and cover with the tossed cabbage mixture. Sprinkle with the warm chicharrones and serve.

YIELD: 4 SERVINGS

Opposite page: Grilled Flank Steak over Mushroom Ceviche

Seafood Frita with Shoestring Fries

Fritas are Cuban-style hamburgers made with chorizo and ground pork flavored with onions and garlic. They're served on small egg bread rolls or burger-style buns, and they're topped with thin julienned fries. You can buy fritas anywhere in Miami, and there are places that specialize in them. I decided to create a healthier frita with seafood that's colored with paprika to make it look authentic.

Shoestring Fries

1 potato, cut into thin shoestrings
Vegetable oil, for deep-frying
Salt to taste

Frita

4 ounces scallops (3 or 4 scallops)
4 ounces shrimp (4 or 5 large shrimp), peeled and deveined
4 ounces calamari
6 ounces fresh tuna
2 eggs
2 tablespoons paprika
2 tablespoons minced garlic
Salt and pepper to taste

1 tablespoon vegetable oil
4 hamburger-style buns, toasted
4 lettuce leaves, shredded
1 beefsteak tomato, cut into 4 slices, 1/2 to 3/4 inch thick

To prepare the fries, place the shoestring potatoes in a pan of water for a few minutes to extract some of the starch. Drain, and pat dry.

Heat the vegetable oil to 400° in a deep fryer or large saucepan and fry the shoestring potatoes until golden brown, 4 or 5 minutes. Drain on paper towels, season with salt, and keep warm.

To prepare the frita, coarsely grind all the seafood in a meat grinder and place in a large mixing bowl. Add the eggs, paprika, garlic, and salt and pepper, and combine thoroughly. Form the mixture into 4 patties.

Heat the oil in a sauté pan or skillet and fry the patties over medium heat until golden brown, about 4 minutes on each side. Drain on paper towels.

Place each patty on a slice of the bread or on a bun and dress with a lettuce leaf and tomato slice. Top with the fries and close the sandwiches with the top halves of the buns.

YIELD: 4 SERVINGS

Opposite page: Seafood Frita with Shoestring Fries

Medianoche Sandwich

This "midnight sandwich," based on the Cuban original, is one of my all-time favorites. The classic version uses ham, roast pork loin, Swiss cheese, pickles, and a dab of mustard on sweet, thick bread. It is called "media noche" because the portion is a little smaller than a regular sandwich, making it the ideal midnight snack. For an alternative presentation, you can serve this on two small rolls. Try using a sandwich press for a deliciously crunchy texture.

8 ounces Swiss cheese, cut into 8 slices
8 slices Medianoche Bread (page 35)
8 ounces ham, cut into 8 slices
8 ounces cooked pork loin (page 127), cut into 8 slices
12 dill pickle chips (optional)
American-style yellow prepared mustard to taste (optional)
3 tablespoons butter, softened
Shoestring Fries (page 61, optional)

Heat a sandwich press or griddle.

Place fig slices of the Swiss cheese on each of 4 slices of the bread. Layer each with 2 slices of ham and then the pork. Dress with the pickle slices and mustard and close the sandwiches with the remaining slices of bread. Spread the outside of each sandwich with a small amount of the butter.

Cook the sandwiches in the press (or on a griddle, covered with a bacon iron) until crispy and golden brown, 5 to 7 minutes.

Cut each sandwich in half on a diagonal and serve with the fries.

YIELD: 4 SERVINGS

Cuban T.B.L.T.

This is the classic B.L.T. (bacon, lettuce, and tomato sandwich), with the addition of turkey. I call it "Cuban" because I make it on a sandwich press. This sandwich is a twist on the popular Cuban pressed sandwich that has ham, pork, and cheese. Making this sandwich is almost an art form, and it's worth the effort!

8 slices bacon (about 8 ounces)
1 pound roasted turkey breast, cut into 32 thin slices
8 slices Cuban Bread (page 29)
8 ounces Swiss cheese, cut into 8 slices
American-style prepared yellow mustard to taste (optional)
3 tablespoons butter, softened
¼ head iceberg lettuce
2 tomatoes, sliced

Heat a sandwich press or griddle.

Cook the bacon in a sauté pan or skillet until crispy, and set aside.

Place 8 slices of the turkey on each of 4 slices of the bread. Layer each with 2 slices of the bacon and 2 slices of the cheese. Dress with the mustard, and close the sandwiches with the remaining slices of bread. Spread the outside of each sandwich with a small amount of the butter.

Cook the sandwiches in the press (or on a griddle, covered with a bacon iron) until crispy and golden brown, 5 to 7 minutes.

Open the sandwiches, add the lettuce and tomato, and then close them again. Cut each sandwich in half on a diagonal and serve immediately.

YIELD: 4 SERVINGS

Avocado Crabwich
with Roasted Garlic Aïoli

This is a great summer sandwich. It was created for an article New York *magazine was publishing on summertime sandwiches, and it was picked as one of the very best.*

1 pound jumbo lump crabmeat, picked through

1 bunch chives, chopped

1/2 red onion, cut into 1/4-inch dice

2 tablespoons diced celery

2 tablespoons peeled, seeded, and diced cucumber

1 tablespoon chopped cilantro leaves

2 tablespoons Dijon mustard

Juice of 1 orange

Juice of 4 limes

1 tablespoon olive oil

Salt and pepper to taste

2 large ready-made corn muffins, sliced in half and toasted

1 avocado, pitted, peeled, and thinly sliced

1 mango, pitted, peeled, and thinly sliced

1/4 cup Roasted Garlic Aïoli (page 9) or mayonnaise

4 slices red onion, for garnish

In a mixing bowl, combine the crabmeat, chives, onion, celery, cucumber, and cilantro.

In a separate bowl, combine the mustard, orange and lime juices, and olive oil and whisk well. Pour over the crabmeat mixture, and toss. Season with salt and pepper.

Place a toasted muffin half on each serving plate. Alternate slices of avocado and mango on top of each muffin, and top with the crab mixture. Spoon or drizzle the aïoli over the crab mixture, and top with slices of red onion.

YIELD: 4 SERVINGS

Pulled Pork and Gouda Baguette
with Papaya-Mustard Salsa

The most important part of this recipe is cooking the pork just right and shredding it by hand. My heritage has a lot to do with my love of pork sandwiches, and there's nothing better than watching a Sunday football game on television with a nice pork sub. In fact, for a Super Bowl party I hosted (when Dallas beat Buffalo for the first time), I made up a bunch of these sandwiches for the 30 or 40 guests I invited over. The sandwiches were a big hit (or maybe it was because most of the people were Dallas fans). Because the pork needs to marinate for at least 12 hours, you need to plan ahead. You can cook and shred the pork ahead of time, and then warm it up when you're ready to make the sandwiches.

3 pounds pork butt, trimmed of excess fat

Marinade

1 large onion, chopped

8 cloves garlic

1/4 cup chopped fresh cilantro leaves

1 tablespoon chopped fresh thyme leaves

1 tablespoon chopped fresh oregano leaves

3 bay leaves

1 tablespoon cumin seeds

2 tablespoons salt

6 peppercorns

1/2 cup distilled white vinegar

1 quart water

2 long, fresh baguette loaves

1 red onion, sliced

24 thin slices Gouda cheese
   (about 12 ounces)

4 tablespoons butter

Papaya-Mustard Salsa (page 42)

Place the pork butt in a deep, oven-proof roasting pan.

To prepare the marinade, place the onion, garlic, herbs, cumin, salt, peppercorns, and vinegar in a blender or food processor and blend or process until smooth.

With the machine running, add the water in a slow stream to make a purée. Pour the purée over the pork, cover the pan tightly, and refrigerate for at least 12 hours.

Preheat the oven to 300°.

Place the pan with the pork and marinade in the oven, and braise until the meat easily pulls apart with a fork, about 2 hours. Remove from the oven and let the pork cool in the marinade. Using 2 forks, shred the pork.

Cut each baguette into three 6-inch-long pieces and then slice each piece open. Add 4 Gouda slices, some onion slices, and some pork. Close the sandwiches with the remaining slices of bread. Spread the outside of each sandwich with a small amount of the butter.

Cook the sandwiches in the press (or on a griddle, covered with a bacon iron) until crispy and golden brown, about 5 minutes per side. (You can also cook the sandwiches in a sauté pan.)

Open the sandwiches and sprinkle some of the salsa on top of the pork. Cut each sandwich in half on the diagonal and serve immediately.

YIELD: 6 SERVINGS

Opposite page: Pulled Pork and Gouda Baguette with Papaya-Mustard Salsa

APPETIZERS

Opposite page: Tasajo Rolls with Chipotle Ketchup

I CAN'T IMAGINE BEGINNING a meal without an appetizer. I enjoy "grazing" through menu first courses, and at the restaurant, we stack different *aperitivos* on plates and serve them in a three-tier stand at the table. As the recipes that follow suggest, I enjoy preparing a variety of culinary styles—from Latin America and beyond—that transcend national borders.

Soups are a perennial favorite and are popular even in tropical regions of the Americas. They can be hearty, nourishing, and inexpensive. I'm endlessly fascinated by the regional specialties whenever I travel to South America. Especially in the poorer regions, soups and stews are often a practical means of cooking tougher cuts of meat.

I like making terrines almost as much as I enjoy eating them. There's an element of showmanship involved, putting together different layers and combinations of color and texture to form an elegant dish. The technique of making terrines may be French, but the recipes here all use popular Latin American ingredients.

Croquetas and empanadas are common snacks and appetizers throughout Central and South America, and the fillings are as limitless as your imagination. The same is true for tamals. It's only in Mexico and parts of Central America that corn masa dough is used; elsewhere, root vegetables and other fillings are the main element. It's fascinating to travel and find that tamals are enclosed by such a wide variety of wrappings—from banana leaves to avocado leaves to dried and fresh corn husks.

Ceviches using citrus juice to marinate and "cook" fish and shellfish are South American in origin and were created by Peruvian Indians centuries ago to preserve seafood, especially as their societies moved inland and farther away from the coast. Chiles and other ingredients were added, and ceviches evolved as their use spread through South and Central America. Still, the most outstanding ceviches I've ever tasted were those in Peru and Ecuador.

Roasted Calabaza Soup

My mother, Gloria, makes a soup that inspired me to create this one, which is made with roasted calabaza, otherwise known as West Indian pumpkin. I've taken her recipe a step further by tossing the pumpkin with spices and butter. Then I roast it in the oven until it turns black, which brings out the full flavor of the pumpkin. This is a great fall or winter soup, when calabaza is in season.

Garnish

1 quart water
1 bay leaf
4 peppercorns
2 cloves garlic
1 small onion, thinly sliced
Salt and pepper to taste
8 ounces skirt steak

1½ to 2 pounds calabaza, West Indian, or regular pumpkin, peeled, seeded, and cut into large chunks
1 large onion, coarsely chopped
1 cup butter
2 teaspoons ground allspice
2 teaspoons ground cinnamon
2 teaspoons ground turmeric
2 teaspoons powdered ginger
⅛ teaspoon ground cloves
½ tablespoon salt
4 quarts Chicken Stock (page 10)
1 tablespoon extra virgin olive oil
1 cup heavy cream
Pepper to taste

Prepare the garnish first. Bring the water to a boil, and add the bay leaf, peppercorns, garlic, onion, and salt and pepper. Lower the heat, add the skirt steak, and simmer, covered, for about 30 minutes. Remove the steak, let cool, and shred into small pieces with 2 forks. Set aside.

Place the pumpkin and onion in a large mixing bowl, and set aside.

Preheat the oven to 350°.

Melt the butter in a sauté pan or skillet, add the spices and salt, and sauté for about 5 to 6 minutes, stirring frequently. Pour this mixture over the pumpkin and onion, and toss well.

Transfer the coated pumpkin and onion to a baking sheet and roast it in the oven until it turns black, about 40 minutes.

In a large saucepan, bring the stock to a simmer. Add the roasted pumpkin mixture and continue to simmer for about 30 minutes.

Meanwhile, heat the olive oil in a sauté pan and sear the shredded steak until browned and crunchy.

Remove the pumpkin mixture from the heat, add the cream, and transfer the soup to a blender or food processor. Purée (in batches if necessary). Season with pepper, and ladle into bowls. Top each serving with about 2 tablespoons of the seared steak.

YIELD: 8 SERVINGS

Gloria's Black Bean Soup

This is another one of my mother's recipes and call me biased, but it's the best around. This is a vegetarian black bean soup, and one of the keys to its success is the quality of the olive oil: use the very best you can find. You can make the soup a day in advance and it will taste even better the next day. This is a no-fail recipe that I know you're going to enjoy.

1 pound dried black beans
3 quarts water
2 bay leaves
1 cup extra virgin olive oil
2 large red bell peppers, seeded
   and chopped
2 shallots, chopped
2 onions, chopped
8 cloves garlic, chopped
1 tablespoon ground cumin
2 tablespoons dried oregano
2 tablespoons chopped fresh oregano leaves
1 1/2 tablespoons sugar
2 tablespoons salt
1 red onion, diced, for garnish
8 ounces sour cream, for garnish (optional)

Place the beans in a nonreactive pan. Cover with the 3 quarts of water, add the bay leaves, and bring to a boil. Reduce the heat and simmer the beans for 2 1/2 to 3 hours, stirring frequently and adding more water if necessary to keep them well covered.

Meanwhile, heat the olive oil in a sauté pan or skillet. Sauté the bell peppers, shallots, and onions over medium heat until the onions are translucent, about 15 minutes.

Add the garlic, cumin, dried and fresh oregano, and sauté for an additional 2 minutes. Remove from the heat and let cool slightly. Transfer to a blender and purée until smooth.

When the beans are almost tender, add the puréed mixture, sugar, and salt to the beans and cook until just tender, 20 to 30 minutes. Adjust the seasonings, garnish with the red onion and sour cream, and serve.

YIELD: 8 TO 10 SERVINGS

Ellyssoise

This soup is dedicated to the memory of my late ex-partner at Yuca, Elly Levy. She had a passion for cooking and eating, and she enjoyed creating recipes at home and bringing them in to me so that I could try them. This cooling soup is one of them, and I've always loved it. It was a big hit, ideal for the hot Florida summers. It's made like the classic French vichyssoise but I substituted yuca for the potato. It's best served chilled, but it can also be warmed. This one's for you, Elly.

1 1/2 pounds yuca, peeled and chopped
2 leeks (white part only), sliced
   (about 1 cup)
1 cup chopped onion
2 cups Chicken Stock (page 10)
1 1/2 cups light cream
Salt and pepper to taste
Pinch mace

Bring a large saucepan of water to a boil. Add the yuca, leeks, and onion, lower the heat, and simmer until tender, about 30 minutes.

Drain the vegetables and transfer to a food processor. Purée until smooth.

Stir in the stock, cream, salt and pepper, and mace. Chill thoroughly before serving.

YIELD: 8 SERVINGS

Opposite page: Gloria's Black Bean Soup

Costa Rican Terrine
with Coconut-Date Vinaigrette

This terrine is called "Costa Rican" because of the hearts of palm, which I associate with that country. I used to call it the Royal palm terrine, since the hearts, coconut, and dates in the recipe are all products of the palm. Cited by Alan Richman, the food editor of GQ magazine, as "ingenious" and one of his favorite dishes, this is one of my favorites too. You can prepare it a couple of days in advance.

Terrine

3 large potatoes (about 1¹/₂ pounds), peeled and cut into large chunks

2 canned chipotle chiles, seeded

2 cups milk

Salt to taste

White pepper to taste

2 tablespoons olive oil

2 teaspoons unflavored gelatin

2 teaspoons cold water

2 tablespoons boiling water

1 can (16 ounces) hearts of palm, drained, and patted dry

Coconut-Date Vinaigrette

1 cup canned coconut milk

¹/₄ cup Coco Lopez

1 cup dark rum

1 cup red wine vinegar

¹/₂ cup sherry vinegar

1 small onion, cut into ¹/₂-inch dice

¹/₄ cup extra virgin olive oil

Salt and pepper to taste

6 dates, pitted and sliced

Garnish

2 cups shaved coconut

8 ounces fresh goat cheese, crumbled

1 pound mixed greens, washed and patted dry

Herb Toast

1 loaf French bread

¹/₂ cup butter

4 cloves garlic, peeled and minced

¹/₄ cup fresh parsley, chopped

Salt to taste

To prepare the terrine, combine the potatoes, chipotles, and milk in a large saucepan. Bring the milk to a gentle boil and cook over medium heat until the potatoes are tender, about 10 to 15 minutes.

Strain the milk from the potatoes and set the potatoes and chiles aside. Return the milk to the pan and gently simmer until it has reduced to about ¹/₃ cup.

Meanwhile, press the potatoes and chiles through a coarse sieve into a large bowl. Stir in the salt, pepper, and olive oil, and set aside.

In a mixing bowl, dissolve the gelatin with the cold water and then stir in the boiling water. Set aside.

Remove the milk from the heat and stir in the dissolved gelatin. Slowly blend this mixture into the potatoes until they are thickly textured.

Line a 9 by 4-inch loaf pan (or other shaped pan, as desired) with plastic wrap; the wrap should extend over the edges of the pan by a couple of inches on all sides. Place one third of the potato mixture in the bottom of the pan and spread out evenly. Add a layer of half of the hearts of palm and then another layer of one third of the potato mixture. Add the remaining hearts of palm and top with the remaining potato mixture. Fold over the plastic wrap to cover the top layer and chill in the refrigerator overnight.

To prepare the vinaigrette, combine the coconut milk, Coco Lopez, rum, vinegars, and onion in a saucepan and reduce over high heat to 1 cup, about 15 minutes. Remove from the heat and let cool.

When cool, whisk in the olive oil and season with salt and pepper. Stir in the dates.

Preheat the oven to 400°. Melt the butter in a small sauté pan; add the garlic and parsley and sauté 2 minutes. Cut the bread into ¹/₂-inch-thick slices. Brush on the garlic mixture and add salt. Place slices on a baking sheet and bake for 5 to 8 minutes, or until browned.

Meanwhile, unfold the top covering of plastic wrap from the terrine, and gently invert the loaf pan on a serving platter, running a knife around the inside edge if necessary. Carefully remove the plastic wrap and cut the terrine into slices. Garnish with the coconut, goat cheese, and greens and serve with the Herb Toast and vinaigrette on the side.

YIELD: 8 SERVINGS

Opposite page: Costa Rican Terrine with Coconut-Date Vinaigrette

Three-Bean Terrine

I created this recipe specifically as a vegetarian appetizer, and it's proved very popular. I serve it with crumbled goat cheese, a splash of sour orange juice, and freshly cracked black pepper, but these garnishes are optional. You can prepare the beans ahead of time.

Beans

$1/2$ cup dried black turtle beans
$1/2$ cup dried white beans
$1/2$ cup dried red kidney beans
3 bay leaves
1 tablespoon olive oil

Sofrito

2 tablespoons olive oil
$2/3$ cup diced white onion
$2/3$ cup diced red bell pepper
2 tablespoons minced garlic
$1/4$ cup fresh cilantro leaves
1 tablespoon unflavored gelatin

Salt and pepper to taste
2 avocados

Garnish

8 ounces fresh goat cheese, crumbled
$1/2$ cup freshly squeezed Seville (sour)
    orange juice, or 6 tablespoons orange
    juice and 2 tablespoons lime juice
Pepper to taste

Place each of the beans in a separate saucepan, cover with water, and soak overnight.

Drain the water from the soaking beans, rinse each separately, and add about 4 cups of cold water (or enough to cover the beans) and 1 bay leaf to each saucepan. Bring each pan to a boil, lower the heat, and simmer for about 40 minutes. Add more hot water as necessary to keep the beans covered.

Remove the beans from the heat and let them cool in their cooking liquid for about 1 hour. Strain off the liquid and rinse the beans in cold water. They should be tender but not falling apart.

Combine all the beans and the olive oil in a large mixing bowl. Refrigerate until needed.

To prepare the sofrito, heat the olive oil in a large skillet. Add the onion and sauté over medium heat for 3 minutes. Stir in the bell pepper and sauté for 5 minutes. Stir in the garlic and sauté for another 3 minutes. Add the cilantro and turn off the heat. Let the mixture cool for 5 minutes.

Transfer the sofrito mixture to a blender and purée on high speed for 1 minute. With the blender running, add the gelatin and purée until incorporated.

Add the puréed sofrito to the beans, and season with salt and pepper.

Grease a 9 by 4-inch loaf pan and line it with plastic wrap. (The wrap should extend over the edges by a couple of inches on all sides.) Pour half of the mixture into the bottom of the pan and spread evenly. Cut the avocados in half, remove the pits, cut off the ends, and separate the flesh halves from the skin. Place the avocado halves on the mixture in the pan and then add the remaining bean mixture. Fold over the plastic wrap to cover the top layer, and chill in the refrigerator overnight.

Unfold the top covering of plastic wrap from the terrine, and gently invert the loaf pan on a serving platter, running a knife around the inside edge to remove it if necessary. Carefully remove the plastic wrap and cut the terrine into slices. Garnish with the goat cheese, orange juice, and pepper.

YIELD: 8 SERVINGS

Tasajo Rolls with Chipotle Ketchup

One of the components of this dish is tasajo, a dried, salt-cured meat like jerky that was traditionally prepared in Spain and Portugal for the winter months. Originally, it was made with horsemeat or beef, but these days it's made only with beef. I prefer South American tasajo, especially the type that comes from Uruguay. Tasajo is available in Latin grocery stores, but you can substitute corned beef, as my friends in Nebraska do. The combination of salty beef and the sweet plantains echoes the traditional Cuban serving style, where tasajo is matched with boniato, the white sweet potato. Pictured on page 66.

8 ounces tasajo or corned beef,
   cut into 1-inch cubes

4 semiripe plantains (yellow with
   some black speckles), peeled and
   cut into 1-inch cubes

1 tablespoon olive oil

1 small onion, cut into $1/2$-inch dice

$1/2$ green bell pepper, seeded and
   cut into $1/2$-inch dice

$1/2$ red bell pepper, seeded and
   cut into $1/2$-inch dice

2 cloves garlic, squeezed through
   a garlic press

2 tablespoons tomato paste

Breading

1 cup all-purpose flour

3 eggs

2 cups cracker meal

Salt and pepper to taste

Vegetable oil, for deep-frying

3 cups Chipotle Ketchup (page 9)

$1/2$ cup sour cream

Place the tasajo in a large saucepan of water and bring to a boil. Reduce the heat and simmer for 40 minutes. Strain off the cooking water and cover with fresh water. Simmer again for 40 minutes. Strain and repeat the process once more.

Remove from the heat and let the meat cool in the water. When cool, strain the meat and shred with 2 forks. Set aside.

Meanwhile, bring a saucepan of water to a boil. Add the plantain cubes, reduce the heat, and simmer for 15 minutes. Remove the pan from the heat, strain, and let the plantains cool.

Heat the olive oil in a sauté pan or skillet, and sauté the onion, bell peppers, and shredded tasajo over high heat for 6 to 7 minutes. Stir in the garlic and tomato paste, and cook for another 3 to 4 minutes. Remove the pan from the heat and let cool.

Once the plantains have cooled, use either a potato masher, fork, or meat grinder to mash them coarsely.

Lay out a 12-inch-long piece of plastic wrap on a flat work surface. Dollop about 6 tablespoons of the mashed plantain onto the plastic wrap and cover with another sheet of wrap. Flatten out the plantain, by hand or with a rolling pin, to form a circle about 5 inches in diameter.

Carefully remove the top sheet of plastic wrap. Spoon about $1/3$ cup of the tasajo mixture onto the middle of the plantain disk and roll up to form a cylindrical (torpedo) shape. Repeat this process with the remaining plantain mixture and tasajo, forming 8 to 10 rolls.

Place the flour, eggs, and cracker meal in separate bowls. Season the flour with some salt and pepper and lightly beat the eggs. Dredge the stuffed plantain rolls first in the flour, then in the egg, and finally in the cracker meal. Cover and refrigerate for at least 1 hour.

In a deep fryer, heat the vegetable oil to 350°. Fry the stuffed plantain rolls until golden brown, 5 or 6 minutes.

Remove the pan from the heat and drain the rolls on paper towels. Serve with the Chipotle Ketchup.

YIELD: 8 TO 10 ROLLS

Ham Croquetas
with Brie and Wilted Kale

Croquetas (Spanish for croquettes) are very popular in many countries, especially when they're made with ham. Part of their appeal, no doubt, is their crispy exterior and their contrasting soft and creamy center. The traditional way of serving croquetas is with slices of cheese and crackers formed into the shape of miniature logs. Instead, I've formed them into pear shapes, an idea I borrowed from classical French cuisine, and added some Brie and wilted kale. At Yuca our guests in particular loved it because it was a familiar dish with an interesting twist.

Croquetas

4 tablespoons butter
2 tablespoons diced onion
1 cup milk
³/₄ cup all-purpose flour
¹/₂ teaspoon salt
¹/₈ teaspoon pepper
¹/₂ teaspoon ground nutmeg
1 tablespoon dry sherry
1 pound smoked boneless ham, ground

Breading

1 cup all-purpose flour
2 eggs
1 cup cracker meal or matzo meal

Canola oil, for deep-frying

Wilted Kale

3 tablespoons olive oil
3 cloves garlic, crushed
8 kale leaves (about 2 cups), julienned

8 ounces Brie cheese, sliced into
    8 to 10 wedges
8 to 10 small kale leaves, for garnish

To prepare the croquetas, heat the butter in a heavy-bottomed saucepan and sauté the onion over high heat until translucent, about 3 to 4 minutes. Set aside.

Place the milk and flour in a blender and blend until combined. Pour this mixture into the sautéed onions and add the salt, pepper, and nutmeg. Simmer over low heat, stirring constantly, until the mixture reaches the consistency of pancake batter.

Remove the saucepan from the heat, add the sherry and ham, and mix well. Pour into a shallow pan and let cool for about 2 hours.

Then, using about 2 tablespoons of the mixture for each croqueta, form into flat-bottomed-pear shapes. (There should be about 16 to 20.)

Place each breading ingredient in a separate small bowl. Lightly beat the eggs. Dredge the croquetas first in the flour, then in the egg, and finally in the cracker meal. Cover and refrigerate for at least 1 hour. The croquetas can also be frozen at this point.

Heat the canola oil in a deep fryer to about 375°. Fry the croquetas until golden brown, about 3 minutes. Drain on paper towels and keep warm in the oven until ready to serve.

Preheat the broiler.

To prepare the kale, heat the olive oil in a sauté pan and sauté the garlic and julienned kale over high heat for about 4 minutes.

Using the broiler, grill the Brie wedges for about 1 minute, until warm and runny. (Alternatively, microwave the Brie for about 15 seconds.)

To serve, place some sautéed kale on each plate and two croquetas over the kale. Garnish with the hot Brie and a kale leaf.

YIELD: 8 TO 10 SERVINGS

Lobster Croquetas
with Roasted Corn and Pepper Salsa

Croquetas were probably originally invented to use up leftovers. (After Thanksgiving, my mother used to make the best turkey croquetas!) We serve a lot of lobsters at my restaurants, and if we have any that aren't quite big enough to serve as the main course, we'll take out the cooked meat and whip up a batch of these croquetas. (If you prefer, you can substitute shrimp for the lobster.)

Croquetas

4 tablespoons butter

2 tablespoons diced onion

3 cloves garlic, squeezed through
    a garlic press

1 cup milk

³/₄ cup all-purpose flour

¹/₂ teaspoon salt

¹/₈ teaspoon pepper

¹/₂ teaspoon ground nutmeg

1 tablespoon cognac

1 pound cooked lobster meat (or shrimp),
    ground

Breading

1 cup all-purpose flour

2 eggs

1 cup cracker meal

Canola oil, for deep-frying

Roasted Corn and Pepper Salsa,
    refrigerated (page 39)

To prepare the croquetas, heat the butter in a heavy-bottomed saucepan and sauté the onion and garlic over medium-high heat until translucent, about 5 minutes. Set aside.

Place the milk and flour in a blender and blend until combined. Pour this mixture into the sautéed onions and add the salt, pepper, and nutmeg. Simmer over low heat, stirring constantly, until the mixture reaches the consistency of pancake batter.

Remove the pan from the heat. Add the cognac and lobster meat and mix well. Pour into a shallow pan and let cool for about 1 hour.

Then, using about 2 to 3 tablespoons of the mixture for each croqueta, shape into small, finger-sized sticks.

Place each breading ingredient into a separate small bowl. Lightly beat the eggs. Dredge the croquetas first in the flour, then in the egg, and finally in the cracker meal. Transfer to a plate, cover, and refrigerate for at least 1 hour or freeze to use at a later time.

Heat about 1 inch of canola oil in a deep fryer to about 375°. Fry the croquetas until golden brown, 3 to 4 minutes. Drain on paper towels. Serve the croquetas with the salsa.

YIELD: 8 SERVINGS

Oyster Croquetas
with Banana-Lentil Salad and
Horseradish Cream

The unusual combination of ingredients in this recipe makes for an outstanding taste sensation with every forkful. You can buy pre-shucked oysters in containers at fish markets, which makes life a lot easier, and wasabi, or Japanese green horseradish, can be found in the Asian foods section of grocery stores. This dish was a favorite of Ruth Reichl's, the New York Times *food critic.*

Horseradish Cream

3 tablespoons prepared horseradish
1 teaspoon wasabi powder
$^1/_2$ tablespoon grated gingerroot
$^1/_2$ cup sour cream
2 tablespoons heavy cream

Croquetas

$^1/_4$ cup olive oil
$^1/_2$ cup diced white onion
$^1/_2$ cup diced red bell pepper
5 cloves garlic, minced
1 pound fresh shucked oysters, drained
1 cup heavy cream
Salt and pepper to taste
$1^1/_2$ cups all-purpose flour

Breading

2 cups all-purpose flour
6 eggs
2 cups cracker meal
Salt and pepper to taste

Canola oil, for deep-frying
Banana-Lentil Salad (page 49)
1 pound mâche
1 container garlic sprouts

Place the Horseradish Cream ingredients in a blender and purée until smooth. Refrigerate.

To prepare the croquetas, heat the olive oil in a heavy-bottomed saucepan and sauté the onion and bell pepper over medium heat for 2 minutes. Add the garlic and oysters, and stirring constantly, cook until the mixture is dry, about 20 minutes. Remove the pan from the heat and let cool.

Transfer the oyster mixture to a food processor and process for 30 seconds. Return the mixture to the pan.

Add the cream and the salt and pepper, and stirring constantly, simmer for 3 minutes. Add the $1^1/_2$ cups flour, $^1/_2$ cup at a time, stirring with a wooden spoon until the mixture forms a ball. Remove from the heat and let cool in the refrigerator for about 2 hours.

Then, using about 2 tablespoons of the mixture for each croqueta, shape into small finger-sized sticks and dust with some flour. Refrigerate for 1 hour (to dry them).

Place the flour and the eggs in separate bowls. Lightly beat the eggs. Season the cracker meal with some salt and pepper and place in another bowl. Dredge the croquetas first in the flour, then in the egg, and finally in the cracker meal. Cover and refrigerate for at least 1 hour, or until ready to fry.

Place about 1 inch of the canola oil in a deep fryer and heat to about 375°. Fry the croquetas until golden brown, 2 to 3 minutes per side. Drain on paper towels. Serve with the Horseradish Cream and Banana-Lentil Salad. Garnish with the mâche and sprouts.

YIELD: 8 TO 10 CROQUETAS

Opposite page: Oyster Croquetas with Banana-Lentil Salad with Horseradish Cream

Conch Tamals with Jalapeño-Cheese Pesto

Unlike most tamal recipes, which use dried corn (masa harina), this one is Cuban-style, made with fresh corn kernels. I've also added a different touch by replacing the traditional pork filling with conch. The flavor and texture proved very popular at Yuca, and it remained on the menu as a fixture.

These tamals are very convenient for entertaining. They can be made ahead of time and frozen, or kept in the refrigerator and then popped in the microwave. In fact, it's not worth making a smaller batch, so you'll probably want to freeze some of them. Likewise, the pesto can be prepared ahead of time and refrigerated.

Jalapeño-Cheese Pesto

$1/4$ cup olive oil

3 tablespoons diced onion

1 tablespoon minced garlic

2 jalapeño chiles, seeded, deveined, and sliced

1 tablespoon ground turmeric

8 ounces queso blanco or Muenster cheese, cut into 1-inch chunks

Sofrito

$1/4$ cup extra virgin olive oil

$1/2$ onion, cut into $1/2$-inch dice

$1/2$ red bell pepper, seeded and cut into $1/2$-inch dice

$1/2$ green bell pepper, seeded and cut into $1/2$-inch dice

4 cloves garlic, minced

3 tablespoons tomato paste

7 to 8 cups fresh corn kernels (from 15 ears), husks reserved

$1/2$ cup fine yellow cornmeal

$1/2$ cup cornstarch

2 tablespoons sugar

Salt to taste

1 pound fresh conch, ground

Garnish

1 large $1/2$-inch-thick slice queso blanco or Muenster cheese (optional)

1 pound whole mixed olives (such as kalamanta, niçoise, and alphonso)

1 bunch fresh parsley, chopped

To prepare the pesto, heat the olive oil in a sauté pan or skillet and sauté the onion, garlic, and jalapeños over medium heat for 5 minutes. Add the turmeric, stir well, and sauté for another 2 minutes.

Transfer the mixture to a food processor, add the queso blanco, and pulse until smooth. Refrigerate.

To prepare the sofrito, heat the olive oil in a large sauté pan or skillet. Add the onion, bell peppers, and garlic, and sauté over medium heat for about 15 minutes, stirring frequently. Stir in the tomato paste and remove the pan from the heat.

Place the corn kernels in a large mixing bowl and stir in the sofrito mixture. Add the cornmeal and cornstarch and mix well. Place small batches of the corn mixture into a food processor or blender and purée until smooth.

Return the purée to the mixing bowl and add the sugar and salt. With a wooden spoon, fold in the ground conch.

Lay 2 of the reserved corn husks end to end. Place $1/2$ cup of the conch filling in a cylinder shape in the middle of the husks. Roll up the husks and tie each end with butcher's twine. Repeat for the remaining tamals.

Bring a large stockpot of salted water to a boil. Add the tamals, lower the heat, and keep at a gentle boil for 1 hour. Drain, and let the tamals cool slightly. Cut the square of cheese into a star (or other) shape and set it on a serving plate. Set the warm tamals, still in their leaves, on the cheese. Place the chilled pesto on the side, garnish with the parsley and olives, and serve.

Note: The tamals may be frozen. Just wrap them tightly and freeze *before* boiling. To cook, place the frozen tamals in a pot of gently boiling water and boil for $1 1/2$ hours.

YIELD: 20 TAMALS

Opposite page: Conch Tamals with Jalapeño-Cheese Pesto

Lamb Picadillo Empanadas with Mint Mojo

Lamb and mint are traditionally paired, and they work well inside these hot, flaky pastries. The dough can be seasoned with crushed black pepper and cumin seeds or rosemary, enhancing the lamb's natural flavor. Freeze any empanadas you have left over.

Mint Mojo

$1/_2$ cup chopped fresh mint leaves
2 cloves garlic
2 tablespoons mint jelly
$1/_3$ cup red wine vinegar
$1/_3$ cup extra virgin olive oil
Salt and pepper to taste

Lamb Picadillo

10 ounces ground lamb
$1/_2$ cup diced white onion
$1/_2$ cup seeded and diced red
    bell pepper
$1/_2$ cup seeded and diced green
    bell pepper
1 tablespoon finely minced garlic
$1/_2$ cup diced tomato
$1/_4$ cup tomato paste
$1/_2$ cup dry red wine
$1/_4$ cup dry sherry
2 tablespoons capers, drained
3 tablespoons minced green olives
Salt and pepper to taste

Empanada Dough (page 83)
Vegetable oil, for frying

Place all of the mojo ingredients in a blender and purée until smooth. Keep refrigerated until needed.

To prepare the picadillo, heat a large sauté pan or skillet over high heat and cook the lamb, stirring occasionally, until it is crumbly and lightly browned, about 10 minutes.

Drain off the fat and return the pan to the heat. Stir in the onion, bell peppers, garlic, and tomato, and sauté for 5 minutes over high heat. In a small bowl, combine the tomato paste, red wine, and sherry, and add this mixture to the pan. Stir in the capers and olives, and cook until the mixture thickens slightly, about 5 minutes. Remove from the heat, season with salt and pepper, and let cool.

Place about 1 tablespoon of the picadillo filling in the center of each dough round, fold over to form a half-moon or turnover, and seal the edges with a fork.

In a large cast-iron pan, heat 1 inch of the oil to 300°. Fry the empanadas until golden brown, 3 to 4 minutes.

YIELD: 15 TO 20 EMPANADAS

Opposite page: Lamb Picadillo Empanadas with Mint Mojo

Malanga Pancakes with Caviar and Vodka-Cumin Sauce

Malanga pancakes are another one of my specialties, and we had them on the menu at Yuca from day one. Malanga has a nutty, earthy yet elegant flavor for a tuber, and therefore is a natural partner for the sophisticated caviar. Malanga is also known as yuatía *in Puerto Rico, and in several Caribbean countries it's given to children and to the sick for its strength-giving, medicinal properties.*

Pancakes

1 $\frac{1}{2}$ pounds malanga, peeled and
    cut into $\frac{1}{2}$-inch dice

2 cups milk

2 cloves garlic

2 eggs

3 tablespoons minced white onion

$\frac{1}{2}$ cup all-purpose flour

$\frac{1}{4}$ cup minced parsley

Salt and pepper to taste

Vodka-Cumin Sauce

$\frac{1}{2}$ cup sour cream

2 tablespoons toasted cumin seeds
    (page 7)

1 tablespoon diced onion

2 tablespoons mayonnaise

Salt and pepper to taste

2 tablespoons vodka

$\frac{1}{4}$ cup vegetable oil

Garnish

2 hard-boiled eggs, finely chopped

$\frac{1}{4}$ cup chopped parsley

1 small red onion, diced

3-ounce jar osetra caviar

$\frac{1}{2}$ cup sour cream

6 to 8 slivers lemon zest

1 bunch chives

To prepare the pancakes, place the malanga and milk in a saucepan. Add enough water to cover the malanga completely and bring to a boil. Reduce the heat, add the garlic, and simmer until the malanga is tender, about 25 minutes.

Drain off the water. Place the malanga and garlic in a mixing bowl and mash well with a potato masher or fork. Add the eggs, onion, flour, parsley, and salt and pepper, and stir to form a batter. Refrigerate for 20 minutes.

Place all the sauce ingredients in a blender and blend for 30 seconds.

Heat the oil in a large sauté pan or skillet over medium-high heat. Drop about 2 tablespoons of the batter into the hot oil and flatten out with the back of a spoon. Cook until golden brown, 5 to 7 minutes per side. Keep warm and repeat for the remaining pancakes. (There should be enough batter for 12 to 16 pancakes.) To prepare the garnish, combine the eggs, parsley, and onion.

To serve, spoon the sauce onto serving plates and add 2 pancakes per plate. Spoon the egg mixture on the pancakes, then top with the caviar. Add a drop of sour cream and garnish with a lemon sliver and chives. Spoon the caviar on top of the pancakes and sprinkle the egg and parsley garnish around the plates.

YIELD: 6 TO 8 SERVINGS

Opposite page: Malanga Pancakes with Caviar and Vodka-Cumin Sauce

Honduran Ceviche

The Central American country of Honduras grows and exports coconuts and is famous for its ceviches, and other seafood snacks—hence the name of this appetizer. This is a refreshing dish, and it's been a favorite at my restaurants. The presentation in coconut shells is dramatic and unusual. Serve this to your friends. (Use only Grade A, sushi-quality tuna for this recipe.)

4 fresh coconuts

Sauce

1 jalapeño chile, chopped, with seeds

2 tablespoons chopped gingerroot

3 tablespoons Oriental fish sauce

1 tablespoon sugar

$^1/_2$ cup freshly squeezed lime juice

1 can (14 ounces) unsweetened coconut milk

$1^1/_2$ pounds fresh tuna, cut into $^1/_4$-inch dice

$^1/_2$ red onion, thinly sliced into half-moons

$^1/_4$ cup shaved coconut

2 tablespoons sliced scallions

1 tablespoon finely chopped chives

3 tablespoons finely chopped fresh cilantro leaves

Garnish

1 batch fried plantains (page 27)

$^1/_2$ cup seeded and diced red bell pepper

bunch watercress, leaves only

2 cups shaved coconut

Using the back of a heavy knife, whack the coconut along its middle while rotating it in your hand, until it splits open. To catch the water, do this over a bowl. Pat the insides of the coconuts dry and refrigerate.

Place the jalapeño, gingerroot, fish sauce, sugar, lime juice, and coconut milk in a blender and purée until smooth. When you are ready to serve, toss with the tuna. Then, at the last minute, sprinkle with the onion, shaved coconut, scallions, chives, and cilantro. Place mixture in the coconut halves and garnish with plantain slices, bell pepper, watercress leaves, and coconut.

YIELD: 8 SERVINGS

Ecuadorian Shrimp Ceviche

This dish was inspired by a trip I made to Ecuador. A friend of mine, Humberto Mata, took me on a tour of the country. We visited a restaurant called La Longita, in the city of Salinas, that only serves ceviches. There were close to twenty different ceviches on the menu, ranging from giant clam to octopus, mussels, and oysters. While we stayed there, I must have tried all of them, and the one that impressed me the most was a tomato-based shrimp ceviche. This recipe echoes both that ceviche and the Ecuadorian custom of placing bowls of popcorn and corn nuts on the table when serving ceviches.

1 pound extra-large shrimp (16 to 20), peeled and deveined

Dressing

1 large tomato, roasted, peeled, seeded, and chopped (page 6)

2 jalapeño chiles, roasted, peeled, seeded, and chopped (page 6)

1 red bell pepper, roasted, peeled, seeded, and chopped (page 6)

$^1/_2$ onion, roasted and chopped

$^3/_4$ cup freshly squeezed lime juice

$^1/_2$ cup freshly squeezed orange juice

$^1/_4$ cup canned tomato juice

1 tablespoon sugar

Tabasco sauce to taste

Salt to taste

1 small red onion, thinly sliced

2 tablespoons chopped chives

2 tablespoons sliced scallions

$^1/_4$ cup chopped fresh cilantro leaves

$^1/_2$ cup freshly made plain, unsalted popcorn

$^1/_2$ cup unsalted corn nuts

Bring a large saucepan of water to a boil. Add the shrimp, turn off the heat, and blanch for no longer than $1^1/_2$ minutes. Remove immediately from the water with a wire-mesh strainer, and transfer to an ice bath to cool. Drain the shrimp thoroughly and place in a mixing bowl.

Place the dressing ingredients in a blender or food processor and purée until smooth. Pour over the shrimp and toss.

Just before serving, toss the ceviche with the red onion, chives, scallions, and cilantro. Transfer to serving plates, sprinkle with the popcorn and corn nuts, and serve.

YIELD: 4 SERVINGS

Opposite page: Honduran Ceviche

Peruvian Black Ceviche

This ceviche was inspired by a black clam ceviche I tried in Peru. When I returned to the United States, I couldn't find a source for black clams, so I came up with the idea of adding squid ink (available at Italian or specialty stores) to the ceviche. Sometimes, I like to add some minced Scotch bonnet chiles for a spicy effect. This dish, like all the other ceviches, makes a delicious low-fat summer appetizer.

1 quart clam juice, Fish Stock (page 10), or water
2$^1/_2$ pounds mixed seafood (clams, scallops, calamari, octopus, mussels, diced fish, etc.)

Dressing

2 roasted jalapeño chiles, chopped, with seeds (page 6)
1 red bell pepper, roasted, peeled, seeded, and chopped (page 6)
$^1/_2$ onion, coarsely chopped
2 teaspoons chopped garlic
2 tablespoons chopped celery

2 teaspoons squid ink (optional)
1$^1/_2$ cups freshly squeezed lime juice
$^1/_2$ cup freshly squeezed orange juice
Salt to taste

3 tablespoons extra virgin olive oil

Garnish

$^1/_4$ cup sliced red onion
2 tablespoons sliced scallions
2 tablespoons finely chopped chives
3 tablespoons chopped cilantro leaves
$^1/_4$ cup diced tomato

In a large saucepan, bring the clam juice, stock, or water to a boil. Add the mixed seafood, and blanch for about 1 minute. Remove immediately with a wire-mesh strainer, and transfer to an ice bath to cool. Drain, and place in a mixing bowl.

Place the jalapeños, bell pepper, onion, garlic, celery, squid ink, juices, and salt in a blender or food processor and purée until smooth. Pour over the mixed seafood and toss gently. Add the olive oil and toss again. Refrigerate for at least 2 hours before serving.

Just before serving, toss the garnish ingredients with the ceviche and transfer to serving plates.

YIELD: 10 SERVINGS

Steamed Clams with Sour Orange Mojo and Chorizo

This is a dish from the Canary Islands, where it's made with tiny clams and pork, or pork sausage, and served with crusty bread in a big bowl. In this version, the clams are cooked in a tangy Seville orange mojo rather than in wine. (If sour oranges are unavailable, you can substitute orange juice mixed with lime juice.)

The chorizo should be the dry, hard type. Serve this dish with Sweet Onion Flatbread (page 31), Patacones (page 28), or slices of a French baguette to sop up the juice!

$^1/_4$ cup extra virgin olive oil
8 cloves garlic, chopped
24 littleneck clams, washed and scrubbed
1 cup freshly squeezed Seville (sour) orange juice, or $^3/_4$ cup sweet orange juice mixed with $^1/_4$ cup lime juice
$^1/_4$ cup minced flat-leaf parsley
$^1/_2$ teaspoon salt

$^1/_4$ teaspoon pepper
12 ounces hard (Spanish) chorizo, finely cut into $^1/_4$-inch dice
6 tablespoons butter

Heat the olive oil in a large sauté pan or skillet and sauté the garlic for 1 minute. Add the clams and $^1/_2$ cup of the orange juice. Cover, and steam the clams until they open, 5 to 8 minutes. Stir in the remaining orange juice, parsley, salt, and pepper, and remove from the heat.

With a slotted spoon, transfer 6 clams to each serving bowl. Add the chorizo to the sauté pan and reheat over high heat. Whisk in the butter and cook for about 1 minute.

Spoon the chorizo and sauce over the clams, and serve with crusty bread.

YIELD: 4 SERVINGS

Sweet Pea Ginger Flan with Fried Oysters

Many people who don't enjoy (or won't eat) raw oysters take enthusiastically to these fried oysters, but you must make the recipe with good-quality fresh oysters. This dish has wonderful, contrasting textures and flavors.

Flan

8 ounces frozen sweet peas (petits pois)
2 tablespoons grated gingerroot
6 eggs
6 tablespoons heavy cream
1/4 cup milk
1/2 teaspoon salt
1/4 teaspoon pepper

Oysters

1 cup matzo meal
1/2 cup all-purpose flour
24 large shucked oysters

3 to 4 cups canola oil, for deep-frying
Salt and pepper to taste
3/4 cup Roasted Garlic Aïoli (page 9)

Preheat the oven to 350°.

Place the peas, ginger, eggs, cream, milk, and salt and pepper in a blender, and purée until smooth. Pour the mixture three quarters full into 6 lightly greased ramekins.

Place the ramekins in a water bath, and fill the water bath with enough hot water to come about halfway up the sides of the ramekins. Bake until the flans are firm in the middle, about 25 minutes.

Meanwhile, to prepare the oysters, combine the matzo meal and flour in a mixing bowl. Dredge the shucked oysters in the mixture.

In a large sauté pan or skillet, heat the canola oil to 350°. Fry 6 to 8 oysters at a time until they are golden brown and crunchy, 4 to 5 minutes. Remove the oysters with a wire-mesh strainer and drain on paper towels. Season with salt and pepper.

To serve, place 4 oysters on each serving plate. Turn out the ramekins onto each plate, running a knife around the edges, if necessary. Serve with the aïoli.

YIELD: 6 SERVINGS

FISH & SEAFOOD ENTRÉES

*Opposite page: Sugarcane Tuna with Malanga Purée and
Dried Shrimp Salsa*

ONE GLANCE AT A MAP is all it takes to understand why fish and seafood are major elements of Latin cuisine. Many countries in Latin America have an extensive coastline. There are hundreds of different types of fish and shellfish commercially harvested in the Atlantic and Pacific oceans and the Gulf of Mexico, and fishing has always been a way of life for those who have inhabited the coastal fringes of these waters. In other regions, especially the landlocked areas of South America, the abundant freshwater lakes and rivers have likewise been important sources of food. This fortunate availability goes a long way toward explaining why Latin Americans enthusiastically embrace fish and seafood in their diets.

If you visit the Caribbean or coastal areas of Central America and countries like Chile and Ecuador, you are likely to be spoiled by the best of the ocean's rich bounty. Likewise, the sights, sounds, and smells of the colorful markets and street stalls selling seafood are reminders of the ocean's proximity.

Fish and seafood are important features of my Nuevo Latino cuisine as well, and the menus at all my restaurants reflect this. People less familiar with Latin food may tend to think of this cuisine as merely pork, rice, beans, or beef cooked with a heavy hand. However, this is far from the truth. With the use of so much seafood and fish, the cuisine can be light and flavorful, healthful and imaginative. This is why at least half of the main courses at my restaurants feature fish and seafood, easily outnumbering meat dishes. Our guests constantly remind us how much they enjoy tasting the flavors and styles of well-prepared seafood recipes from other cultures and cuisines.

Ropa Nueva with Saffron Rice and Peas

Named after the Spanish/Cuban classic Ropa Vieja, a shredded beef dish made with skirt steak and served with rice, this version uses skate (or ray), a sweet, firm fish. This dish goes well with black beans, and you can substitute plain white rice (page 8) for the saffron rice, if you prefer.

2½ pounds skate wing, peeled and boned

1 tablespoon olive oil

1 teaspoon minced garlic

2 tablespoons crushed red pepper flakes

Salt to taste

Saffron Rice

1½ cups long-grain white rice

3 tablespoons Annatto Oil (page 8)

1 cup diced onion

2 cloves garlic, minced

1 tablespoon saffron threads

2½ cups cold water

½ tablespoon salt

1 cup sweet peas (petits pois)

Sauce

3 tablespoons olive oil

1 cup diced white onion

2 tablespoons minced garlic

2 red bell peppers, seeded and finely julienned

½ cup dry white wine

1 cup Fish Stock (page 10)

½ cup tomato paste

1 bay leaf

¼ cup sliced scallions

Preheat the oven to 350°.

Place the skate in a mixing bowl, add the olive oil, garlic, crushed red pepper, and salt, and gently toss. Transfer to a baking sheet and bake for 20 to 25 minutes. Remove from the oven and let cool for 1 hour.

Meanwhile, rinse the rice under cold, running water until the water runs clear. Heat the oil in a heavy-bottomed saucepan and sauté the onion, garlic, and saffron over medium-high heat for 3 to 4 minutes, stirring occasionally.

Add the water and salt, bring to a boil, and add the rice. Continue boiling, uncovered, until the rice has absorbed almost all of the water.

Reduce the heat to the lowest possible setting, cover the pan, and cook for another 20 minutes. Turn off the heat and fluff the rice with a fork. Add the peas, cover, and let sit for 5 minutes before serving.

To prepare the sauce, heat the olive oil in a large skillet and sauté the onion, garlic, and bell peppers over medium-high heat for 5 minutes. Add the wine, stock, tomato paste, and bay leaf, and bring to a boil. Reduce the heat and simmer for 5 to 7 minutes.

Shred the cooled skate with 2 forks and add to the skillet. Add the scallions and cook for 3 minutes.

To serve, place the rice on serving plates and top with the skate and sauce.

YIELD: 6 SERVINGS

Banana Leaf-Wrapped Pompano with Crab Topping and Hearts of Palm Salad

This recipe is my spin on the classic French technique of preparing fish en papillote (wrapped in parchment paper and cooked in the oven). In this recipe, the pompano is cooked in banana leaves—a traditional tropical technique. The pompano, with its tasty, mild and delicate flesh, is one of the most elegantly textured fish you can buy. Unfortunately, it is also one of the most expensive.

Crab Topping

8 ounces lump crabmeat, picked through

2 small tomatoes, finely diced

I small red onion, finely diced

I red bell pepper, seeded and julienned

2 scallions, finely sliced

2 tablespoons chopped fresh cilantro leaves

2 tablespoons freshly squeezed lime juice

I tablespoon extra virgin olive oil

Salt and pepper to taste

Pompano

$1/4$ cup extra virgin olive oil

2 white onions, julienned

I large red bell pepper, seeded and julienned

3 cloves garlic, minced

2 large banana leaves, cut into six 18 by 18-inch squares

6 pompano fillets (6 to 7 ounces each), with skin on

2 teaspoons paprika

Salt and pepper to taste

$1/4$ cup dry white wine

Salad

I pound cooked fresh hearts of palm, or I can (16 ounces)

$1/4$ cup freshly squeezed lemon juice

2 tablespoons extra virgin olive oil

2 tablespoons chopped fresh parsley, for garnish

Combine the crab topping ingredients in a mixing bowl and mix well. Refrigerate.

Preheat the oven to 500°.

To prepare the pompano, heat a large skillet over high heat and add the olive oil. Sauté the onions, bell pepper, and garlic for 3 minutes. Remove the skillet from the heat and let cool.

Lay the banana leaf squares on a work surface. Place the cooked onion mixture in the center of each leaf and spread out with a spoon to an area of 3 inches by 5 inches. Sprinkle the pompano fillets with the paprika and season with salt and pepper. Place each fillet on top of the cooked onion mixture. Fold in the sides of each banana leaf (not too tightly) to form an envelope.

Place the wrapped pompano in a lightly greased baking pan and add the wine. Bake in the oven until the banana leaves become brown around the edges, 20 to 30 minutes.

Meanwhile, cut the hearts of palm into $1/2$-inch pieces and toss with the lemon juice and olive oil in a mixing bowl.

Remove the banana leaf envelopes from the oven and arrange on serving plates. Slit the banana leaves open, spreading out the leaves to expose the baked fish. Top with the reserved crab mixture and garnish with the parsley. Serve with the hearts of palm salad.

YIELD: 6 SERVINGS

Opposite page: Banana Leaf-Wrapped Pompano with Crab Topping and Hearts of Palm Salad

Cumin- and Pumpkin Seed–Dusted Grouper with Poblano Mashed Potatoes

Grouper is a type of warm-water sea bass with lean, firm flesh. It's a favorite of mine, and I especially like cooking with the flavorful black grouper. The coating of fragrant cumin and crunchy pumpkin seeds in this recipe adds a delicious and special touch.

Poblano Mashed Potatoes

1½ pounds potatoes, peeled and cubed

1 small canned chipotle chile, seeded

2 quarts milk

6 tablespoons butter

1 large poblano chile, roasted, peeled, seeded, and cut into ½-inch dice (page 6)

Salt and pepper to taste

Fish

2 tablespoons toasted cumin seeds (page 7)

4 tablespoons unsalted pumpkin seeds

6 black or regular grouper fillets (about 7 ounces each)

Salt to taste

¼ cup extra virgin olive oil

Place the potatoes and the chipotle chile in a large saucepan and cover with the milk. Bring to a boil, reduce the heat, and simmer until tender, 20 to 30 minutes.

Drain the milk from the potatoes and reserve. Mash the potatoes and chipotle with a potato masher, fork, or mixer, adding the butter 1 tablespoon at a time. Mix in ¾ to 1 cup of the reserved cooked milk to achieve the desired texture. Fold in the poblano chile and season with salt and pepper. Keep warm.

Meanwhile, combine the cumin and pumpkin seeds in a spice mill or grinder and coarsely grind. Transfer to a platter. Salt the grouper fillets and firmly press *one side only* into the seed mixture.

Preheat the oven to 400°.

Heat a large ovenproof skillet over medium-high heat, and add half of the olive oil. Place 3 fillets, coated side down, in the hot oil and sear until slightly browned, about 2 minutes.

Turn the fillets over and sear the other side for 2 minutes. Transfer the pan to the oven and bake for 5 minutes. Repeat for the remaining fillets.

Serve the grouper with the mashed potatoes.

YIELD: 6 SERVINGS

Roasted Yellowtail Snapper
with Potatoes, Olives, and Tomatoes

This is a fail-safe, simple recipe for yellowtail snapper, which is a game fish with a delicate flaky texture. You can prepare everything ahead of time and keep it in the refrigerator until your guests arrive. When you buy the yellowtail, ask to have it cleaned and scaled, if possible. Red snapper can be substituted. It is a bit firmer-fleshed than its cousin, the yellowtail.

1 yellowtail snapper (about 3 pounds), cleaned and scaled, with skin on

1 teaspoon salt

Vegetables

2 baking potatoes, peeled and cut into $1/2$-inch-thick slices

3 tomatoes, halved and sliced

1 cup pitted alphonso or niçoise black olives

1 teaspoon chopped oregano leaves

$1/4$ cup olive oil

4 cloves garlic, sliced

$1/4$ cup dry sherry

Salt and pepper to taste

1 tablespoon chopped parsley, for garnish

Preheat the oven to 450°.

Make three slits, about 4 inches long, along each side of the yellowtail, about 3 inches apart. Sprinkle the yellowtail with the salt, and place in a deep-sided baking dish.

Place all of the vegetable mixture ingredients in a mixing bowl and mix well. Pour all around the yellowtail in the baking dish.

Bake until the fish flakes easily, 30 to 35 minutes. Remove the dish from the oven and serve the fish whole at the table, or transfer the fish and vegetables to individual serving plates. Sprinkle with the parsley and serve.

YIELD: 4 SERVINGS

Tipi Tapa Snapper and Gallo Pinto

This is a classic Nicaraguan dish that originates in the region near the Tipi Tapa River. The traditional recipe uses corvina, *a meaty white fish, but I'm substituting snapper. (You can also use grouper, halibut, or another firm, white-fleshed fish.) The dusting for the snapper is an unusual mixture that adds an attractive color and flavor to this delicate fish.*

Gallo Pinto is a Nicaraguan recipe for red beans and rice cooked together. It's the perfect accompaniment for the snapper.

Gallo Pinto

$^1/_2$ cup dried red kidney beans, soaked overnight

2 bay leaves

1 teaspoon dried oregano

4 slices bacon, cut into $^1/_2$-inch dice

3 tablespoons diced onion

3 tablespoons seeded and diced red bell pepper

$^1/_2$ cup diced ham

3 cloves garlic, squeezed through a garlic press

2 tablespoons tomato paste

1 teaspoon ground cumin

Salt to taste

3 cups water

2 cups long-grain white rice

Sauce

$^1/_4$ cup extra virgin olive oil

2 white onions, halved and thinly sliced into half-moons

4 tomatoes, halved and sliced

8 cloves garlic, thinly sliced

$^1/_4$ cup cider vinegar

1 cup Fish Stock (page 10)

$^1/_2$ cup tomato ketchup

Salt and pepper to taste

1 tablespoon chopped fresh cilantro leaves

Coating

$^1/_4$ cup all-purpose flour

3 tablespoons cocoa powder

2 tablespoons pure red chile powder

1 teaspoon garlic powder

$^1/_4$ cup cornstarch

Salt and pepper to taste

6 snapper fillets (6 to 7 ounces each), with skin on

$^1/_2$ cup vegetable oil, for frying

To prepare the Gallo Pinto, place the beans and their soaking water in a large, ovenproof pot or saucepan, adding more water if necessary to cover. Add the bay leaves and oregano, and bring to a boil. Reduce the heat and simmer the beans until just tender, 1 to $1^1/_2$ hours.

About 15 minutes before the beans have finished cooking, sauté the bacon in a dry skillet over medium-high heat until crispy. Stir in the onion, bell pepper, and ham, and sauté for another 5 minutes. Stir in the garlic, tomato paste, cumin, and salt, and cook for another 2 or 3 minutes.

Preheat the oven to 325°.

When the beans are tender, stir in the sautéed bacon mixture and the water. Bring to a boil and add the rice. Reduce the heat to medium and cook for 10 minutes, until almost all of the water has evaporated.

Remove the saucepan from the heat and place a sheet of foil or a lid over the pan. Transfer to the oven to bake for 25 minutes.

To prepare the sauce, heat the olive oil in a large skillet and sauté the onions and tomatoes over high heat for about 4 minutes, stirring continuously. Add the garlic and cook for 5 minutes.

Stir in the vinegar, fish stock, and ketchup, and continue cooking for 10 minutes over high heat. Remove from the heat and season with salt and pepper. Stir in the cilantro and keep warm.

Sift the coating ingredients onto a large platter. Dredge the snapper fillets in the coating, covering evenly and shaking off any excess.

In a large skillet, heat the oil to 350°. Add the snapper and sear until cooked through, about 4 minutes on each side. Remove the snapper and drain on paper towels.

Remove the Gallo Pinto from the oven and fluff with a fork before serving.

To serve, place the snapper in the center of each serving plate. Spoon the sauce over the fish and serve with the Gallo Pinto.

YIELD: 6 SERVINGS

Avocado- and Pistachio-Crusted Gulf Snapper with Black Bean Sauce

This is a recipe I designed for Delta Airlines' first-class in-flight meal service. I've met travelers from around the world who've told me they've enjoyed this dish—talk about a global village! One of these travelers, Michael Stipe, who is the lead singer of the rock group R.E.M., had this dish on a Delta flight and then came by the restaurant because he enjoyed it so much.

Black Bean Sauce

8 ounces dried black beans, soaked overnight

1 bay leaf

2 tablespoons extra virgin olive oil

3 tablespoons diced white onion

3 tablespoons seeded and diced red bell pepper

1 teaspoon minced garlic

1 teaspoon dried oregano

1 teaspoon ground cumin

Salt and pepper to taste

Crust

2 semiripe Haas avocados, peeled, pitted, and cut into $1/2$-inch dice

1 teaspoon minced garlic

$1/2$ cup shelled green pistachios

3 slices pumpernickel bread, diced

1 tablespoon chopped fresh cilantro leaves

1 tablespoon chopped fresh parsley

3 scallions, finely sliced

3 tablespoons butter, softened

Salt and pepper to taste

6 snapper fillets (7 to 8 ounces each), with skin on

$1/4$ cup dry sherry

To prepare the sauce, place the beans in a large saucepan with 3 cups of their soaking water. Add more of the water as necessary to keep the beans covered. Add the bay leaf and bring to a boil. Reduce the heat and simmer the beans for about $1 1/2$ hours.

Meanwhile, heat the olive oil in a skillet and sauté the onion, bell pepper, and garlic over medium heat for 10 minutes. Stir in the oregano and cumin at the last minute.

Remove the skillet from the heat and let cool. Transfer the mixture to a food processor or blender, and purée until smooth.

Stir the purée into the beans and cook until tender, another 30 minutes. Season with salt and pepper, and keep warm.

Meanwhile, place the crust ingredients in a large mixing bowl and toss gently. Let stand for 10 minutes.

Preheat the oven to 400°.

Place the fish, skin side down, in a lightly greased baking pan. Spread the crust on top of each fillet and pour the sherry around the fish. Bake for 20 minutes.

Spoon $1/4$ cup of the bean sauce onto the center of each serving plate and place the snapper on top of the sauce. Serve with white rice (page 8), if desired.

YIELD: 6 SERVINGS

The Original Plantain-Coated Mahimahi

Whenever I can, I head out to the open ocean in a sport boat and cast my line for game fish. One of my biggest thrills was successfully landing a 25-pound mahimahi. It's one of my favorite fish to cook and eat, and it's perfect for this recipe (although you can use any kind of white, firm-fleshed fish, such as grouper, sea bass, cod, or halibut).

I came up with the idea for crusting fish with plantains about 4 or 5 years ago. Since then, I've seen versions on a number of different menus. Imitation is the sincerest form of flattery, they say, and I'm proud of the recipe. This dish has even made it onto television, when I prepared it for a PBS program. My co-conspirator in devising this recipe was my former sous chef, Andrew DiCataldo.

Tamarind Tartar Sauce

1 cup mayonnaise

2 tablespoons freshly squeezed lime juice

1 tablespoon grated onion

$^1/_4$ cup diced green and black olives

$^1/_4$ cup tamarind juice

Fufu

6 slices bacon (about 6 ounces), diced

1 small onion, cut into $^1/_2$-inch dice

3 ripe plantains, peeled and cut into 1-inch cubes (page 7)

Plantain Crust

4 cups canola oil, for deep-frying

4 green plantains, peeled and thinly sliced (page 7)

1 cup all-purpose flour

4 eggs, lightly beaten

6 mahimahi (dolphin) or halibut fillets (7 to 8 ounces each)

Salt and pepper to taste

Garlic Plantain Chips, for garnish (page 27)

Place the mayonnaise, lime juice, onion, olives, and tamarind juice in a mixing bowl and mix well. Refrigerate.

To prepare the fufu, fry the bacon in a hot, dry skillet until crisp, 4 or 5 minutes. Transfer to a plate and set aside. Add the onion to the skillet and sauté for another 2 minutes. Remove from the heat and let cool.

Bring a saucepan of water to a boil. Add the ripe plantains, reduce the heat, and simmer until soft, about 15 minutes. Drain, transfer the plantains to a mixing bowl, and mash with a potato masher or fork. Add the sautéed onion and bacon, and keep warm.

To prepare the crust, in a saucepan or deep fryer heat the oil to 350°. Add the plantain slices and fry until golden brown, 3 to 4 minutes. Remove the slices with a wire-mesh strainer or slotted spoon, drain on paper towels, and let cool.

Transfer the fried plantain to a food processor, process to a coarse grind, and put in a bowl. Place the flour and eggs in separate bowls.

Season the mahimahi fillets on both sides with salt and pepper and dredge *on one side only* first in the flour, then in the egg, and finally in the ground plantains. Let dry for 1 to 2 minutes.

Strain the frying oil and transfer $^1/_4$ cup to a large clean skillet. Over medium-high heat, fry the fillets, coated side first, for 4 to 5 minutes per side, depending on thickness.

Place the fufu on serving plates. Arrange the mahimahi on top of the fufu, and top each serving with 2 tablespoons of the tartar sauce. Garnish with the plantain chips.

YIELD: 6 SERVINGS

Opposite page: The Original Plantain-Coated Mahimahi

Sugarcane Tuna with Malanga Purée and Dried Shrimp Salsa

It's amusing how some dishes come about. A food writer, who was interviewing me by telephone, once asked if I used sugarcane in the kitchen. I said I used sugarcane juice for marinades a lot and he replied, "Okay, what else do you do with it?" At this point, I got an idea and asked him to call me back the next day. I went straight to the store, bought some sugarcane, and cut it into thin sticks. When I skewered some chicken with it, I discovered that it actually tenderized the meat. Next, I tried it with tuna, and, sure enough, the cane stick sweetened the meat and made it softer in texture. The food writer got his story, and this dish has been a hit ever since. Pictured on page 92.

I stick sugarcane (about 12 inches long), quartered lengthwise
4 1-inch-thick center-cut tuna loins (6 to 7 ounces each)

Malanga Purée

1½ pounds malanga, peeled and cubed
2 cups milk
3 cloves garlic
2 ounces fresh goat cheese
Salt and pepper to taste

Coconut Glaze

1 cup canned coconut milk
2 star anise
1 small stick cinnamon
¼ cup soy sauce
½ cup Myer's dark rum
½ tablespoon peppercorns
¼ cup Coco Lopez

1 tablespoon canola oil
Salt to taste
Dried Shrimp Salsa, refrigerated (page 40)

With a sharp knife, make a point at one end of the sugarcane skewers. Poke the tip of the knife into the cane a few times to release some of the juices. Insert a skewer into the side of a tuna loin, through the center, and out the other side. Repeat for the remaining skewers and tuna. Keep refrigerated while preparing the malanga and the glaze.

Place the malanga, milk, and garlic in a saucepan and top with enough water to cover the malanga. Bring the mixture to a boil. Reduce the heat and simmer until the malanga is tender, 30 to 35 minutes.

Drain the malanga, reserving ½ cup of the milk. Mash the goat cheese into the cooked malanga with a potato masher or fork, adding the reserved milk a bit at a time, until the mixture is smooth but still thicker than regular mashed potatoes. Add the salt and pepper. Keep warm.

For the glaze, place the coconut milk, anise, cinnamon, soy sauce, rum, peppercorns, and Coco Lopez in a saucepan. Over high heat, reduce the liquid by half, 10 to 15 minutes. Strain into a bowl and set aside.

Heat a sauté pan or skillet over high heat, and add the canola oil. Salt the tuna lightly and sear in the pan on all sides, 1 to 2 minutes per side.

Pour the glaze over the tuna, letting it adhere to the fish. Turn the tuna to coat on both sides. Sear the tuna to medium-rare; however, if you prefer well-cooked tuna, finish for 5 to 10 minutes in an oven set at 400°.

Serve the tuna beside the malanga purée and sprinkle the salsa around the plate.

YIELD: 4 SERVINGS

Grilled Dolphin with Mango-Cachucha Relish

Whenever we put dolphin on the menu, we inevitably get quizzed about it. No, it's not the playful ocean-going mammal, but another name for mahimahi (which is the Hawaiian name for the fish). This is a simple barbecue dish for the backyard.

Mango-Cachucha Salsa

2 semiripe mangoes, peeled, pitted, and cut into $1/4$-inch dice

$1/3$ cup freshly squeezed lime juice

4 cachucha chiles, seeded and julienned

1 tablespoon chopped fresh cilantro leaves

1 red bell pepper, seeded and cut into $1/4$-inch dice

Coating Mixture

4 cloves garlic, squeezed through a garlic press

$1/4$ cup extra virgin olive oil

$1/4$ cup freshly squeezed lime juice

1 tablespoon chopped fresh cilantro leaves

Salt and pepper to taste

8 dolphin (mahimahi) fillets (about 7 or 8 ounces each)

Prepare the grill.

Combine the mangoes, lime juice, chiles, cilantro, and bell pepper in a mixing bowl and mix well. Refrigerate.

In a separate mixing bowl, combine the garlic, olive oil, lime juice, cilantro, and some salt and pepper. Place the dolphin fillets in the mixture, turning to coat well on both sides.

Grill the coated fish until cooked to the desired doneness, about 3 minutes per side.

Transfer the dolphin to serving plates and serve with the salsa and mashed potatoes or white rice (page 8).

YIELD: 8 SERVINGS

Swordfish Escabeche and Tostones

I'm often asked what distinguishes escabeche dishes from ceviches. Both preparations involve cooking or preserving in an acidic pickling liquid or marinade. Whereas escabeches involve cooking and then marinating, ceviches usually use a marinade that itself "cooks" the fish or seafood. In Cuban cuisine, escabeche is traditionally made with kingfish. In many other parts of Latin America, vegetables, eggs, and poultry as well as seafood are prepared en escabeche.

Tostoneras, hinged wooden presses for making tostones (fried green plantains), are available at Latin markets.

6 boneless swordfish loins
   (about 7 to 8 ounces each)
Salt and pepper to taste

Coating

¼ cup extra virgin olive oil
1 tablespoon chopped fresh rosemary
   leaves
3 cloves garlic, squeezed through
   a garlic press

Escabeche

1 cup red wine vinegar
3 cups Fish Stock (page 10)
3 tablespoons tomato paste
¼ cup extra virgin olive oil
1 red bell pepper, seeded
   and julienned
1 yellow bell pepper, seeded
   and julienned
1 green bell pepper, seeded
   and julienned
1 small red onion, julienned
3 cloves garlic, minced
¼ cup capers, drained
½ cup sliced alphonso or
   niçoise black olives, plus additional
   whole olives, for garnish
Salt and pepper to taste

½ cup Roasted Garlic Aïoli (page 9)
1 teaspoon capers, drained

Tostones

3 cups vegetable oil
3 green plantains, peeled and
   cut into 1-inch slices (page 6)
Salt to taste
6 lime slices, for garnish

Season the swordfish with salt and pepper. Mix the coating ingredients in a large mixing bowl, add the swordfish, and thoroughly cover with the coating.

Heat a large, dry sauté pan or skillet over medium-high heat and sear the coated swordfish for about 4 to 5 minutes on each side, depending on the thickness of the fillets. Transfer to a large, shallow baking pan.

To prepare the escabeche, reduce the vinegar in a sauté pan or skillet over high heat for about 3 minutes. Stir in the stock and tomato paste, and reduce by half over medium-high heat, 15 to 20 minutes.

Meanwhile, heat the olive oil in a separate sauté pan and sauté the bell peppers, onion, and garlic for 2 to 3 minutes over high heat. Turn off the heat, stir in the capers and olives, and season with salt and pepper.

Pour this mixture over the seared swordfish fillets, and add the reduced vinegar-fish stock mixture. Cover the pan and keep at room temperature for 6 to 8 hours before serving, turning the fillets occasionally.

Prepare the aïoli and fold in the capers. Refrigerate.

To prepare the tostones, heat the oil in a large skillet to 350°. Fry the plantain slices in the hot oil until they start to become somewhat soft, 6 to 8 minutes. Remove with a wire-mesh strainer or slotted spoon and drain on paper towels. Let cool slightly.

Using a tostonera, the bottom of a small plate, or a very strong spatula, firmly press each plantain slice to flatten it out. Return the flattened plantains into the hot oil and refry until crispy, 2 minutes. Drain on paper towels. Sprinkle the tostones with salt and keep warm.

To serve, place a swordfish fillet on each serving plate and spoon some of the escabeche mixture over the top. Serve with the warm tostones and a dollop of the aïoli. Garnish with the lime slices.

YIELD: 6 SERVINGS

Opposite page: Swordfish Escabeche and Tostones

Rum-Marinated Swordfish with Black Bean Muñeta and Saffron Mayo

This is one recipe that's actually easier to perfect at home than in a restaurant, because it's important that the swordfish be marinated for no less and no more than 30 minutes. If it's marinated longer, the rum marinade begins to break down the fish, ruining the texture and overwhelming its flavor. (In a restaurant kitchen, it's more difficult to marinate small batches of fish and to keep track of them than at home.)

The muñeta (puréed black beans) can also be served as a side dish with many other fish or meat dishes; it makes a good substitute for mashed potatoes. For variety, use white beans in this recipe. The Roasted Corn and Pepper Salsa (page 39) is an ideal accompaniment for this dish.

Black Bean Muñeta

12 ounces dried black beans,
    soaked overnight
2 bay leaves
1 teaspoon dried oregano
1/2 cup olive oil
1 large onion, cut into 1/2-inch dice
2 tablespoons minced garlic
1 teaspoon ground cumin
1 tablespoon chopped fresh
    oregano leaves
Salt and pepper to taste

Rum Marinade (page 13)
6 3/4-inch-thick swordfish loins
    (about 8 ounces each)
1/2 cup Saffron Mayonnaise (page 9)
2 tablespoons canola oil
Salt to taste

To prepare the black bean muñeta, place the beans and their soaking water in a large saucepan. Add the bay leaves and dried oregano, and bring to a boil. Reduce the heat and simmer until the beans are very tender, 2 1/2 to 3 hours. Add more water as necessary to keep the beans covered.

Meanwhile, heat the olive oil in a sauté pan or skillet. Add the onion and garlic, and sauté over high heat until tender, about 5 minutes. Add the cumin and oregano, and sauté for another 2 or 3 minutes. Season with salt and pepper, and set aside.

Prepare the marinade and marinate the swordfish in the refrigerator for exactly 15 minutes per side.

Meanwhile, prepare the mayonnaise and keep refrigerated.

When the beans are cooked, drain all but 1 cup of the cooking liquid and reserve. In small batches, add the beans and cooked onion mixture to a food processor and purée until smooth. If the mixture becomes too thick, add a small amount of the reserved cooking liquid until it reaches the desired thickness. (It should be a little loose, like mashed potatoes.) Keep warm.

Heat a skillet or sauté pan and add the oil. Remove the swordfish from the marinade and sprinkle with some salt. Sear the swordfish over high heat for about 4 minutes per side.

Place the beans in the center of each serving plate. Serve the swordfish on top of the beans, and spoon the mayonnaise around the beans.

YIELD: 6 SERVINGS

Opposite page: Rum-Marinated Swordfish with Black Bean Muñeta and Saffron Mayo

Mango- and Mustard–Glazed Salmon with Calamari Rice

At Yuca, I prepared this dish on a cedar wood plank soaked in citrus rinds and cooked in the oven. "Plank" cooking is a method used for centuries by native Indians of the Americas, but it's somewhat complicated for the home cook. Therefore, in this recipe we grill the salmon, which works just as well. The Mango-Mustard Glaze can be prepared ahead of time and stored in the refrigerator for up to 5 days; the rice can be made in advance but is best eaten the same day.

Mango-Mustard Glaze

1 ripe mango, peeled, pitted, and puréed
(about ³/₄ cup)

5 ounces (¹/₂ can) mango nectar

1 tablespoon mustard seeds

¹/₄ cup Dijon mustard

2 tablespoons American-style
prepared yellow mustard

2 tablespoons prepared brown mustard
(Gulden's)

2 tablespoons cider vinegar

Salt to taste

Calamari Rice

2 tablespoons extra virgin olive oil

3 tablespoons diced white onion

3 tablespoons seeded and diced
red bell pepper

2 cloves garlic, squeezed through
a garlic press

1 teaspoon ground cumin

2 bay leaves

4 cups Fish Stock (page 10)

Salt to taste

8 ounces (2 cans) calamari in its ink

2¹/₂ cups long-grain white rice

Salmon Coating

2 tablespoons vegetable oil

Salt and pepper to taste

3 tablespoons julienned fresh basil leaves

6 salmon fillets (6 to 7 ounces each),
with skin on

3 cups watercress or mâche

12 thin mango slices, rolled, for garnish

Place the glaze ingredients in a saucepan and simmer for 25 minutes. Remove from the heat and let cool. Transfer to a blender or food processor, and purée. Refrigerate.

Preheat the oven to 300°.

To prepare the rice, heat the olive oil in a heavy-bottomed, ovenproof saucepan or skillet, and sauté the onion and bell pepper for 3 minutes. Stir in the garlic, cumin, bay leaves, stock, salt, and calamari, and bring to a boil.

Add the rice and simmer for 10 minutes, until most of the liquid has evaporated. Cover the pan with foil or a lid, transfer to the oven, and bake for 25 minutes.

Prepare the grill.

Combine the coating ingredients in a mixing bowl. Coat the salmon in the mixture on both sides. Grill for 3 to 4 minutes per side; just before removing the salmon, brush liberally with the glaze.

Serve the salmon with the rice and the watercress on the side. Garnish with the mango slices.

YIELD: 6 SERVINGS

Opposite page: Mango- and Mustard–Glazed Salmon with Calamari Rice

Softshell Crabs with
Guiso de Maíz and Chipotle-Potato Mash

I wish it could be summer all year round, so that I could enjoy softshell crabs more often. The season for them—May through August—is all too brief for my liking. The combination of the crabs, the fresh corn, and the yellow potatoes is like summer on a plate.

The guiso de maíz is a traditional Cuban recipe (guiso means "stew"). This recipe is my grandmother's; she often made it for me when I was a kid. Even then, I couldn't understand why she put lard in it, but I don't want to change a good thing and the unique flavor, so I've kept it in the recipe. It's a rare dish of mine in calling for lard; there are only a couple of others in my entire repertoire. You can substitute olive oil and it'll taste fine, but it won't come out quite the same.

Guiso de Maíz

$1/2$ cup lard
I cup diced white onion
$1/2$ cup seeded and diced red bell pepper
$1/2$ cup seeded and diced green
    bell pepper
I tablespoon finely minced garlic
8 ounces boneless ham,
    cut into $1/2$-inch dice
8 ounces pork shoulder,
    cut into $1/4$-inch dice
4 cups fresh corn kernels
    (from 6 to 8 ears)
I pound yellow potatoes, peeled and
    cut into $1/2$-inch dice
I quart water
I quart Lobster Stock (page 11)
3 tablespoons tomato paste
Salt and pepper to taste

Chipotle-Potato Mash

2 pounds yellow potatoes, peeled
    and cubed
5 cloves garlic
3 dried chipotle chiles, seeded
    and crumbled
I cup milk
5 tablespoons butter, softened
Salt and pepper to taste

Crab Coating

I cup all-purpose flour
I tablespoon salt
I tablespoon pepper
I tablespoon paprika
I tablespoon dried ancho chile powder,
    or pure red chile powder
I teaspoon dried oregano
I teaspoon ground cumin
I tablespoon garlic powder

3 cups canola oil, for frying
12 softshell crabs, cleaned
12 to 18 chives, for garnish

To prepare the Guiso de Maíz, melt the lard in a large saucepan. Stir in the onion, bell pepper, garlic, ham, and pork, and sauté for 20 minutes over medium-high heat, stirring frequently.

Add the corn kernels and cook for another 10 minutes, stirring occasionally. Add the potatoes, water, and stock, and whisk in the tomato paste. Season with salt and pepper. Reduce the heat and simmer for I hour, until the potatoes are tender. Keep warm.

Meanwhile, to prepare the mash, place the potatoes, garlic, chipotles, and milk in a saucepan. Add enough water to completely cover the potatoes by I inch. Cover the pan and cook over medium heat until the potatoes are tender, 20 minutes.

Remove from the heat and drain, reserving $1/2$ cup of the cooking liquid. Mash with a potato masher or fork, adding the butter I tablespoon at a time. Season with salt and pepper, and add as much of the reserved cooking liquid as needed to achieve the desired thickness.

Sift all the crab coating ingredients into a large mixing bowl. In a large skillet, heat the oil to about 400°. Dredge the crabs in the coating mixture and fry in the oil for about $1 1/2$ minutes on each side. Remove and drain on paper towels.

Serve some of the chipotle mashed potato in the center of each serving plate. Spoon the Guiso de Maíz around the potatoes. Cut the crabs in half and stand up in the mashed potatoes, with the legs sticking out. Garnish with the chives.

YIELD: 6 SERVINGS

Opposite page: Softshell Crabs with Guizo de Maíz and Chipotle Potato Mash

Enchilado de Camarones

This is another classic dish that my grandmother used to make. My Aunt Teresa made it too, and I can remember running into her house when I was very young, and smelling this dish as it cooked on the stove. The word enchilado, *a Cuban seafood dish in a spicy tomato-based sauce, is not to be confused with* enchilada, *the Mexican stuffed and rolled tortilla usually served with chile sauce. Make this dish the next time you think "Shrimp Creole."*

Perfect White Rice (page 8)

$^1/_4$ cup extra virgin olive oil

$^1/_2$ onion, cut into $^1/_2$-inch dice

$^1/_2$ cup cachucha chiles, seeded and minced

2 jalapeño chiles, seeded and minced

1 red bell pepper, seeded and minced

1 green bell pepper, seeded and minced

3 cloves garlic, minced

1 cup dry white wine

2 tablespoons tomato paste

1 cup Fish Stock (page 10)

3 pounds large shrimp (60 to 75), peeled and deveined

3 tablespoons chopped cilantro leaves

3 tablespoons chopped parsley

Salt and pepper to taste

Prepare the rice and keep warm.

Heat the olive oil in a large sauté pan or skillet, and sauté the onion, chiles, and bell peppers over medium-high heat until the onion is translucent, about 5 minutes. Add the garlic and sauté for another minute.

Deglaze the pan with the wine. Reduce the heat to medium, stir in the tomato paste and stock, and continue cooking for 20 minutes, stirring occasionally.

Add the shrimp, cilantro, parsley, and season with salt and pepper. Cook for about 5 minutes. Serve immediately on a bed of white rice.

YIELD: 6 SERVINGS

Sango Que Te Mata

This is a classical Ecuadorian dish. The title means "Sango that'll kill you" (Sango being the name of the sauce), but it's also a play on words because this is a dish that was introduced to me by my dear friend, Humberto Mata, during a trip to his country. It's a stew of green plantains, peanuts, and shrimp that's served with rice. In Ecuador, it's brought to the table in individual casserole-type clay pots, so if you own any, they'll add to the authenticity. You'll find that the chile and green tomato salsa is perfect with this stew. Sometimes, when I'm in the mood, I'll add a tablespoon of mustard seeds to boost the salsa a bit.

Sango Sauce

2 quarts Lobster Stock made with shrimp (page 11)

2 tablespoons extra virgin olive oil

1/2 cup diced onion

1/2 red bell pepper, seeded and cut into 1/2-inch dice

4 cloves garlic, squeezed through a garlic press

3 green plantains, peeled and finely grated (page 9)

1/2 cup smooth peanut butter

1/4 cup chopped cilantro leaves

2 pounds large shrimp (40 to 50), peeled and deveined

Salt and pepper to taste

3 tablespoons extra virgin olive oil

Perfect White Rice, kept warm (page 8)

Cachucha, Scotch Bonnet, and Green Tomato Salsa (page 39)

To prepare the sauce, bring the stock to a boil in a heavy-bottomed saucepan and reduce over high heat to 1 quart.

Meanwhile, heat the olive oil in a small skillet and sauté the onion over low heat for 4 minutes. Add the bell pepper and garlic, and sauté for another 4 minutes.

Transfer to a food processor or blender and purée until smooth. Stir into the reduced stock together with the plantains and peanut butter. Simmer until the sauce is thick enough to coat the back of a spoon, 30 to 40 minutes. Stir in the cilantro and remove from the heat. Purée again, and keep warm.

Season the shrimp with salt and pepper. Heat the olive oil in a large skillet and sauté the shrimp over high heat for 3 minutes, turning to cook evenly. Be sure not to overcook the shrimp, or they will become tough.

Stir in the sauce and cook another 5 minutes.

To serve, spoon some rice onto each serving plate and top with 7 or 8 shrimp. Ladle the sauce over the shrimp and rice. Garnish the edges of each plate with the salsa.

YIELD: 6 SERVINGS

POULTRY & MEAT ENTRÉES

Opposite page: Patria Pork with Boniato Purée and Black Bean Broth

IT WAS THE SPANISH who brought cattle, pigs, sheep, and goats to South America, and the culinary impact of these domesticated animals was enormous. The newly introduced livestock flourished throughout the Caribbean and Central and South America. The popularity of pork throughout Latin America mirrors the enthusiasm with which the Spanish introduced and consumed it. In many countries, including Cuba, pork is traditionally the meat of choice for Sunday dinner and special occasions.

Although my mom exposed us to a wide variety of foods, I think her specialty was *arroz con pollo* ("chicken with rice"). My entire family loved it. Like other poultry and fowl, chicken and turkey are extremely popular in Latin American kitchens, not only because they are relatively inexpensive, but also because they are wonderfully versatile.

Some of the dishes in this chapter appear on the menus at my restaurants. The rest are simply my favorites. The Guava-Glazed Barbecued Ribs (page 128), for example, are a big hit with young and old guests alike and grilling them brings back my fondest memories. You will be transported to a different country with almost every recipe in this chapter. I know you'll enjoy the trip with each bite.

Asturiano Chicken with Clams and Blood Sausage

Asturia is a province in Spain where they cook chicken wings, clams, and blood sausage in a broth. Blood sausage (also known as black sausage) is not always easy to find, but a well-stocked Latin market should have some on hand. Small clams like littlenecks are ideal for this dish, but Manila clams are also fine to use. This warming, hearty dish is particularly well suited for a chilly winter evening.

Perfect White Rice (page 8)

2 tablespoons olive oil
1 chicken (about 3 pounds), with
    backbone removed, cut into 8 pieces,
    and fat trimmed
Salt and pepper to taste
2 tablespoons paprika
1 small white onion, cut into 1/2-inch dice
3 cloves garlic, minced
1 red bell pepper, seeded and julienned

1 jalapeño chile, seeded and minced
3 tablespoons capers, drained
3 tablespoons sliced alphonso or
    niçoise black olives
4 ripe tomatoes, chopped
1 cup dry red wine
1 pound blood sausage,
    cut into 1-inch slices
20 littleneck or Manila clams, scrubbed
2 tablespoons minced parsley

While the rice is cooking, heat the olive oil in a large saucepan. Season the chicken with salt, pepper, and paprika, and place in the pan. Sear over high heat until browned, about 3 minutes on each side.

Stir in the onion, garlic, bell pepper, jalapeño, capers, and olives. Add the tomatoes, stir well, and sauté for 5 minutes. Add the wine, sausage, and clams, reduce the heat, and simmer the clams, covered, for 5 minutes, checking to see when the clams open. When they do, season with salt and pepper, add the parsley, and simmer for another 2 minutes. (Discard any clams that do not open.)

Place the rice in serving bowls, and serve with the stew.

YIELD: 6 SERVINGS

Latino-Style Chicken Fricassee

I was raised on chicken and turkey fricassees, yet I still enjoy eating them. This is a no-nonsense kind of dish. You can just pop it in the oven and let it cook without having to worry about it. To create the most flavorful fricassee, use the driest white wine available.

1/4 cup extra virgin olive oil
1 chicken (about 3 pounds),
    cut into 8 pieces, with backbone
    and skin removed
1 small onion, halved and sliced
    into half-moons
3 cloves garlic, minced
1 cup dry white wine
1 red bell pepper, seeded and

cut into 1/2-inch dice
2 ripe tomatoes, seeded and
    cut into 1/2-inch dice
3 tablespoons capers, drained
1/4 cup slivered alphonso or
    niçoise black olives
2 russet potatoes, peeled and cubed
Salt to taste
Perfect White Rice, kept warm (page 8)

Heat the olive oil in a large skillet and sear the chicken pieces over medium-high heat until browned on all sides. Stir in the onion and garlic, and cook for 2 minutes.

Add the wine, bell pepper, tomatoes, capers, olives, and potatoes, cover with a lid, and reduce the heat. Simmer until tender, 20 to 25 minutes. Season with salt and serve over the rice.

YIELD: 4 SERVINGS

Chicken Criollo with Malanga-Goat Cheese Purée

This recipe calls for marinating the chicken for 24 hours, so that the chicken absorbs the intense flavor of the cure. In fact, the longer you leave the chicken in the marinade, the more the cure will infuse the meat. I've left the chicken sitting in the marinade for up to 2 days, and the flavor just gets better and better. It also makes the chicken succulently moist. I prefer to bone the entire chicken, which makes it easier to eat, and although it's best to leave the skin on for grilling purposes, you can remove it after it's cooked.

3 chickens (about 3 pounds each), halved and boned
5 cups Fresh Cilantro Adobo (page 11)

Malanga-Goat Cheese Purée

2 pounds malanga, peeled and cubed
1 quart milk
5 ounces fresh goat cheese
Salt and pepper to taste

Red Malanga Chips (page 28 and see instructions at right)

Place the chicken in $3^1/_2$ cups of the adobo (reserve the remaining $1^1/_2$ cups) and coat well. Cover with plastic wrap and refrigerate for at least 24 hours.

To prepare the purée, place the malanga in a saucepan and add the milk. Add enough water to completely cover the malanga, and bring to a boil. Reduce the heat, and simmer the malanga until tender, about 40 minutes.

Meanwhile, prepare the grill.

Drain the milk from the malanga, reserving 1 cup of the milk for mashing. Mash the malanga with a potato masher or fork, adding the goat cheese and enough of the reserved milk to create a thick but creamy consistency. Season with salt and pepper and keep warm.

Prepare the malanga chips as the recipe directs, but omit the beet juice. Remove the chicken from the adobo and drain; discard the adobo used for the marinade. Grill the chicken over a hot flame for 7 to 10 minutes on each side. To serve, spoon the purée onto individual plates. Spoon some of the reserved adobo around the purée. Place 1 chicken half over the purée on each plate. Top each chicken half with the remaining adobo. Serve with the malanga chips.

YIELD: 6 SERVINGS

Prosciutto-Wrapped Chicken with Guava Vinaigrette

Bob Rosar is the executive chef for Cater Air, a company that prepares in-flight meals for airlines, and a friend of mine. We met through the American Airlines Chefs Conclave, a group of professional chefs from across the country. We get together from time to time to discuss food trends and menus for the airline. Bob spent a few days in the kitchen with me and got a feel for my cuisine and the ingredients I use. This is a dish he came up with while we were working together.

Guava Vinaigrette

$^1/_2$ cup canned guava nectar
$^1/_4$ cup cider vinegar
1 tablespoon honey
1 teaspoon ground cayenne pepper
2 tablespoons extra virgin olive oil
12 ounces prosciutto, cut into 24 slices

$1^1/_2$ pounds chicken tenderloins (about 12 tenderloins) or boned chicken breasts cut into 12 2-ounce strips
2 tablespoons extra virgin olive oil
10 ounces mixed greens (such as baby spinach, Bibb lettuce, radicchio, red leaf lettuce, and arugula), rinsed well

To prepare the vinaigrette, place the guava nectar, vinegar, honey, cayenne, and olive oil in a blender and purée.

Wrap 2 slices of prosciutto around each chicken strip.

Heat the olive oil in a large skillet and sear the wrapped chicken over high heat on all sides, until browned. Reduce the heat to medium, and continue cooking for about 5 minutes, turning occasionally.

Arrange the greens on serving plates. Place the prosciutto-wrapped chicken on top of the greens. Serve the vinaigrette in small serving bowls at the side of each plate as a dip for the salad and chicken.

YIELD: 4 SERVINGS

Opposite page: Chicken Criollo with Malanga—Goat Cheese Purée

Grilled Chicken Breasts with White Bean and Asparagus Salad

This is a very simple dish that I like to serve in the fall. Although I think of it as a seasonal recipe, the peak season for asparagus runs through the spring and early summer, so you should consider serving it then as well. This is another dish that calls for the chicken to be marinated overnight.

Red Tomato Marinade (page 12)

6 boneless skinless chicken breasts (7 to 8 ounces each)

10 ounces dried white navy beans, soaked overnight

2 bay leaves

1 small red onion, halved and thinly sliced

1 teaspoon minced garlic

2 tablespoons chopped parsley

1/4 cup balsamic vinegar

3 tablespoons olive oil

Salt and pepper to taste

2 bunches young asparagus (about 30 spears), bottoms trimmed off, and peeled

Bowl of ice water

Marinate the chicken breasts, covered, in the refrigerator overnight. Turn over the chicken breasts occasionally.

The next day, drain the beans and place in a saucepan with enough fresh water to cover by at least 1 inch. Add the bay leaves and bring to a boil. Reduce the heat, and simmer the beans until very tender, 30 to 35 minutes.

Prepare the grill.

Drain the beans, transfer to a large mixing bowl, and let cool for about 10 minutes. Mix in the onion, garlic, parsley, vinegar, olive oil, and salt and pepper, and let cool in the refrigerator.

Remove the chicken breasts from the marinade, drain, and pat dry. Cook on the hot grill for about 4 minutes on each side, depending on size and thickness.

Bring a saucepan of salted water to a boil and cook the asparagus for 2 minutes. Remove the asparagus from the pan and shock in a bowl of ice water.

On each plate arrange the 5 spears of asparagus like the spokes of a wheel. Spoon the bean salad in the center of the "wheel," covering the bottoms of the asparagus. Place the chicken breasts at the side of the beans.

YIELD: 6 SERVINGS

Fried Chicken Breasts with Cachucha Salsa and Garlic Mashed Potatoes

This is a simple recipe that combines the crispness of the warm, fried chicken with the chilled salsa. Fried chicken may sound common, but with the cachucha salsa and seasoned flour it becomes Nuevo Latino!

Buttermilk Marinade (page 13)
6 boneless skinless chicken breasts
    (7 to 8 ounces each)
Cachucha, Scotch Bonnet, and
    Green Tomato Salsa (page 39)

Garlic Mashed Potatoes

2 pounds russet potatoes, peeled
    and cubed
6 to 8 cloves garlic
1 cup milk
1 to 2 cups water
1 cup butter
Salt to taste

Seasoned Flour (page 8)
1 cup canola oil, for frying

Marinate the chicken breasts, covered, in the refrigerator overnight. Turn over the chicken breasts occasionally.

The next day, prepare the salsa.

Place the potatoes in a saucepan with the garlic and milk, and add enough water to cover the potatoes. Bring to a boil, reduce the heat, and simmer until tender, 30 minutes. Drain the potatoes, reserving 1 cup of the cooking liquid. Mash the potatoes with a potato masher or fork, adding the butter a bit at a time. Slowly add some of the reserved cooking liquid while continuing to mash, until the potatoes are very smooth. Season with salt and keep warm.

While the potatoes are cooking, remove the chicken from the marinade, drain, and let sit for 5 minutes. Dredge the chicken breasts in the seasoned flour, coating thoroughly.

In a deep, heavy-bottomed skillet, heat the oil to 350°. Fry the coated chicken breasts until golden brown, 3 minutes on each side.

To serve, place the mashed potatoes in the center of each serving plate. Place the chicken breasts on top the potatoes, and top them with the salsa.

YIELD: 6 SERVINGS

Duck Breasts Escabeche
with Roasted Blue Potatoes

Loosely translated, escabeche *means "pickled" in Spanish. In this recipe, the duck should marinate in the escabeche sauce overnight, or preferably for 24 hours. This dish can be prepared ahead of time and should be served at room temperature, which makes it an ideal picnic item or summer dish.*

6 skinless boneless duck breasts
Salt and pepper to taste
3 tablespoons olive oil

Escabeche Sauce

1 cup extra virgin olive oil
1 cup julienned red onion
1 cup julienned red bell pepper
1 cup julienned yellow bell pepper
1 cup julienned green bell pepper
3 tablespoons capers, drained
$^1/_2$ cup chopped alphonso or
    niçoise black olives
2 ripe tomatoes, chopped
1 cup sherry vinegar
2 tablespoons tomato paste
$^1/_2$ cup ketchup
1 teaspoon chopped garlic
1 teaspoon ground cayenne pepper
1 tablespoon salt

12 to 18 fresh rosemary sprigs,
    for garnish

2 pounds large blue or russet potatoes
1 tablespoon extra virgin olive oil
Salt and pepper to taste

Season the duck with salt and pepper. Heat the 3 tablespoons of olive oil in a skillet and sear the duck over high heat until nicely browned, 2 minutes per side. Set aside.

To prepare the duck in escabeche sauce, place the cup of olive oil, onion, bell peppers, capers, olives, and tomatoes in a large mixing bowl. Add the seared duck and mix together. Put the vinegar, tomato paste, ketchup, garlic, cayenne, and salt in a blender and purée. Add this to the duck breast mixture and mix well. Cover the bowl tightly with foil or plastic wrap and store in the refrigerator overnight.

To prepare the potatoes, preheat the oven to 375°. Place the potatoes in a mixing bowl and toss them with the olive oil and some salt and pepper. Prick the potatoes with a fork and place them on a large sheet of aluminum foil. Wrap up the foil around them and bake for 45 to 60 minutes. Remove the potatoes from the oven and let cool thoroughly before serving.

Slice the potatoes, if desired, and serve with the duck and escabeche sauce at room temperature. Garnish with rosemary sprigs.

YIELD: 6 SERVINGS

Opposite page: Duck Breasts Escabeche with Roasted Blue Potatoes

Guava-Glazed Roast Turkey
with Chorizo Corn Bread Stuffing

Just after Thanksgiving a few years ago, a regular customer of mine told me, "I'm a big fan of your guava barbecued ribs, and I want to tell you, I made up some of your guava glaze and brushed it on our turkey. We didn't need any cranberry sauce, it came out so great." This inspired me to fine-tune this recipe, and here's the result. The stuffing is a third-generation recipe handed down through the family from my mother's grandfather.

Chorizo Corn Bread Stuffing

2 cups Chicken Stock (page 10)

$1/4$ cup olive oil

1 small onion, cut into $1/2$-inch dice

3 cloves garlic, minced

$1/2$ cup diced celery

$1/2$ cup diced carrot

1 red bell pepper, seeded and cut into $1/2$-inch dice

2 cups fresh corn kernels (from 4 ears)

1 pound chorizo sausage or salami, cut into $1/2$-inch dice

1 recipe Cuban Corn Bread (page 32), crumbled

Salt and pepper to taste

1 bunch scallions, chopped

2 tablespoons chopped fresh thyme leaves

1 turkey (12 to 14 pounds), washed and giblets removed

2 cups guava marmalade

To prepare the stuffing, reduce the chicken stock in a saucepan over medium-high heat to 1 cup. Meanwhile, heat the olive oil in a heavy-bottomed sauté pan or skillet. Add the onion, garlic, celery, carrot, bell pepper, corn, and chorizo, and sauté for 10 minutes, stirring occasionally.

Stir in the crumbled corn bread and reduced chicken stock until thoroughly mixed together. Season with salt and pepper and stir in the scallions and thyme. Remove the pan from the heat and set aside until you are ready to stuff the turkey.

Preheat the oven to 300°.

Generously sprinkle the cavity and skin of the turkey with salt. Fill the cavity with the stuffing, packing it as loosely as possible. Place the turkey in a roasting pan and roast for about 5 hours (for a 12-pound turkey), or 25 minutes per pound. (If you have extra stuffing, bake it with the turkey in a separate buttered pan for the last hour of the turkey's cooking time. Or, bake separately at 325° for 40 to 60 minutes.)

Baste the roasting turkey with its drippings every hour. After 3 hours, brush the turkey completely with the gauva marmalade. After 4 hours, brush again, and repeat 30 minutes later.

Remove the turkey from the oven and let rest for 20 minutes before carving.

Serve the turkey with the side dishes and vegetables of your choice, or, the traditional Cuban way, with black beans and white rice (page 8).

YIELD: 8 TO 10 SERVINGS

Cuban-Style Roast Suckling Pig

In Cuba, this dish is traditionally served on New Year's Day. In this tradition, as in the Hawaiian luau, the pig is usually covered with banana leaves and cooked over a coal fire in a pit that's dug in the backyard. Because this method is not easy to do at home, the recipe below uses a small suckling pig that will fit in the oven, yet deliver the same delicious flavor. Ask your butcher to split the pig for you. Don't be afraid to give this recipe a try—cooking a whole small pig is like cooking a whole turkey.

Marinade

Juice of 30 Seville (sour) oranges, or
    juice of 20 limes and 8 regular oranges
    (7 to 8 cups)
Cloves from 6 heads of garlic, minced
1 cup minced fresh oregano leaves
5 tablespoons salt

1 whole suckling pig
    (about 12 pounds), split
Lime, Garlic, and Oregano Mojo
    (page 43)

Combine the juice, garlic, oregano, and salt in a mixing bowl. Transfer to a large, deep roasting pan and place the pig, belly down, into the pan. Thoroughly coat the pig with the marinade, massaging it in. Let sit in the marinade overnight. Baste the pig occasionally.

Preheat the oven to 275°.

Remove the pig from the marinade and place it on a large baking sheet. Cover the pig's ears, snout, and tail with aluminum foil. Place the baking sheet in the oven and cook for 4 to 4$^1/_2$ hours (20 minutes per pound).

Remove the foil when you take the pig out of the oven. Let it rest for 15 to 20 minutes before carving. Serve with the mojo, and some black beans and rice (page 8).

YIELD: 8 SERVINGS

Roasted Pork Loin with Nicaraguan Vigoron Salad

This is a straightforward recipe that yields delicious results. The pork should be marinated for at least 12 hours, and preferably overnight. The salad is my version of the Nicaraguan vigoron.

2$^1/_2$ cups Red Tomato Marinade
    (page 12)
2 pork tenderloins (about 1 pound each),
    trimmed of silver skin
1 tablespoon extra virgin olive oil
Nicaraguan Vigoron Salad (page 58)
Perfect White Rice (page 8)

Combine the marinade and the tenderloins in a large bowl. Cover, and let marinate in the refrigerator overnight.

Remove the tenderloins from the marinade, pat dry, and bring to room temperature.

Preheat the oven to 350°.

Heat the olive oil in a large skillet and sear the tenderloins on all sides over high heat until browned, about 3 minutes per side. Transfer to a roasting pan and bake for 7 minutes.

Remove the pork from the oven and let it rest briefly. Slice the tenderloins and serve with the vigoron and rice.

YIELD: 4 SERVINGS

Guava-Glazed Barbecued Ribs with Boniato Fries

This is a recipe I developed years ago at The Wet Paint Cafe in Miami Beach with the help of Bernie Matz. It has evolved quite a bit since then, and has become one of my signature dishes. There are several schools of thought on barbecue sauce, partly divided along regional lines. Some folks like it hot; others like it vinegary or mustardy. This Guava Barbecue Sauce is more on the sweet side, but I think you will find it delicious. You can make the barbecue sauce ahead of time, and the ribs should marinate overnight.

Marinade

$1/2$ onion, cut into $1/2$-inch dice
2 tablespoons chopped fresh cilantro leaves
2 tablespoons chopped fresh oregano leaves
1 teaspoon ground cumin
1 teaspoon pepper
$1/2$ cup red wine vinegar
6 cloves garlic, minced
Salt to taste
2 bay leaves
$1/2$ cup water

4 racks pork baby back ribs

Guava Barbecue Sauce

1 can (9 ounces) guava marmalade
2 tablespoons tomato paste
2 tablespoons dark corn syrup
2 tablespoons molasses
3 tablespoons distilled white vinegar
1 teaspoon Colman's mustard powder
1 teaspoon ground cumin
1 teaspoon minced onion
1 teaspoon minced garlic
$1/4$ cup dry sherry

Boniato Fries

$1 1/2$ pounds boniato, peeled
4 cups vegetable oil, for deep-frying
Salt to taste

Roasted Corn and Pepper Salsa (page 39)

To prepare the marinade, place the onion, cilantro, oregano, cumin, pepper, vinegar, garlic, and salt in a food processor or blender and purée until smooth. Transfer to a mixing bowl, add the bay leaves, and stir in the water until incorporated. Add the ribs to the bowl, turning them to completely coat. Cover and marinate in the refrigerator overnight. Turn the ribs occasionally.

Combine all the barbecue sauce ingredients in a saucepan and bring to a simmer over medium heat. Reduce the heat and simmer for 2 hours. Turn off the heat and let cool.

Preheat the oven to 550°.

Transfer the ribs and marinade to a roasting pan and bake in the oven for 20 minutes. Remove the ribs from the marinade, discard the marinade, and let the ribs cool to room temperature. Make incisions down the side of each bone, taking care not to cut all the way through.

Prepare the grill.

Brush the ribs with the guava barbecue sauce and grill or return the ribs to the oven for 10 minutes. Turn the racks over frequently and baste with more of the sauce.

Meanwhile, to prepare the fries, cut the boniato into shoestrings, preferably with a mandoline slicer. In a deep fryer or large saucepan heat the oil to 350° and fry the boniato in 2 batches until golden brown, 8 to 9 minutes. Drain on paper towels and sprinkle with salt.

Serve the ribs with the boniato fries and corn salsa. Serve the remaining barbecue sauce on the side.

YIELD: 4 SERVINGS

Opposite page: Guava-Glazed Barbecued Ribs with Boniato Fries

Patria Pork with Boniato Purée and Black Bean Broth

This is another of my signature dishes that won a prize in a professional competition sponsored by the Pork Council. It's a simple recipe adapted from the Cuban classic, vaca frita ("fried cow"). I used to call it "twice-cooked pork" because it's first braised and then pan-crisped, but it became a favorite at the restaurant and the title "Patria Pork" stuck. Each element of the recipe—the pork, the beans, the boniato, and the garnish—can be made in advance and stored until needed. I prepared the dish in a 3- or 4-inch ring mold to add to its beauty. Pictured on page 116.

Marinade

1/2 cup chopped white onion
1/4 cup distilled white vinegar
1/4 cup chopped fresh cilantro leaves
2 tablespoons chopped fresh thyme leaves
2 tablespoons chopped fresh oregano leaves
8 cloves garlic
3 bay leaves
1 tablespoon cumin seeds
2 tablespoons salt
Pepper to taste
4 cups water

5 pounds boneless pork butt, trimmed of excess fat

Black Bean Broth

1 pound dried black beans
1 teaspoon chopped fresh oregano leaves
1 teaspoon ground cumin
2 bay leaves
2 quarts water
6 red bell peppers, seeded
2 white onions
20 cloves garlic

Boniato Purée

2 pounds boniato, peeled and cut into 1/2-inch dice
4 cups milk
2 cups water

2 tablespoons extra virgin olive oil
8 cachucha peppers, seeded and minced
1/2 cup chopped fresh cilantro leaves
Juice of 4 limes

Garnish

1 boniato
3 cups vegetable oil

Using a mandolin slicer, cut the boniato into strips. Heat the oil to 350° in a deep fryer or heavy-bottomed saucepan. Immediately add the boniato strips. Deep-fry until golden, 3 to 4 minutes (cooking in batches if necessary). Remove the strips with a wire-mesh strainer and drain on paper towels.

Place all the marinade ingredients except the water in a food processor or blender. With the motor running, add the water gradually to form a purée.

Place the pork in a large ovenproof dish or nonreactive pan and pour the marinade over the pork. Cover, and marinate in the refrigerator for 12 hours, or overnight. Turn the pork occasionally.

Preheat the oven to 300°.

Place the pork and marinade in the oven and bake until the pork is very tender and almost falling apart, about 3 hours. Remove the pork and let cool slightly. Using 2 forks, shred the pork.

Meanwhile, to prepare the black bean broth, place the beans, oregano, cumin, bay leaves, and water in a large saucepan, adding more water, if necessary, to cover the beans. Bring to a boil, reduce the heat, and simmer for 2 hours, adding enough water to keep the beans covered. Place the bell peppers, onions, and garlic through a juicer and add the juice to the saucepan. Simmer for another 30 minutes. Strain the liquid into a clean saucepan and simmer for another 20 minutes.

To prepare the boniato purée, place the boniato, milk, and water in a large saucepan and bring to a boil. Lower the heat and simmer until tender, about 1 hour. Drain the boniato and mash with a fork. Add a touch of milk, if necessary, to keep the boniato moist.

While the boniato is cooking, heat the olive oil in a large skillet and add the shredded pork, peppers, and cilantro. Cook over medium-high heat, stirring continuously, until crispy. Add the lime juice at the last minute.

Spoon some mashed boniato onto each serving plate. Serve the pork on top of the boniato and ladle some of the black bean broth around it.

YIELD: 8 TO 10 SERVINGS

Braised Short Ribs with Chipa Guasu

This recipe will be a lot easier to make if you ask your butcher to remove the rib meat from the bones. Although short-rib meat is mostly lean, the surface fat gives it a deliciously rich, full flavor when cooked. However, if you prefer, you can trim off most of the fat. Chipa Guasu is a favorite Paraguayan recipe that can be made in advance and reheated before serving.

2 cups Seasoned Flour (page 8)
4 pounds short ribs, meat removed from
    the bones and cut into 3-inch strips
I cup olive oil
2 cups chopped onions
I cup sliced celery
I cup sliced carrots
3 bay leaves
I0 to I2 peppercorns
I bottle (750 ml.) dry red wine
I cup Demi-Glace (page I0)

Chipa Guasu

I tablespoon extra virgin olive oil
I cup finely diced onion
3 cups fresh corn kernels (from 6 ears)
6 eggs, separated
$\frac{1}{2}$ cup milk
I tablespoon sugar
I teaspoon salt
3 ounces mozzarella cheese, grated

Preheat the oven to 400°.

Place the seasoned flour on a plate and dredge the rib meat to coat with the flour. Heat the olive oil in a large skillet and cook the meat in batches over medium-high heat until well-browned on all sides, 4 to 5 minutes.

Transfer the seared rib meat to a roasting pan. Add the onions, celery, carrots, bay leaves, peppercorns, and wine, and add water, if necessary, to completely cover.

Braise in the oven for $1\frac{1}{2}$ to 2 hours. Remove the roasting pan from the oven, remove the meat from the pan, and set aside. Strain the braising liquid into a large saucepan, discarding the vegetables. Add the demi-glace to the braising liquid, return the meat to the pan, and simmer the liquid for 20 minutes.

While the rib meat is braising, prepare the chipa guasu. Heat the olive oil in a sauté pan or skillet and sauté the onion over medium-low heat until translucent, about 5 minutes. (Do not let the onion brown.) Place the corn kernels, egg yolks, milk, sugar, and salt in a blender and blend for I minute. Transfer the mixture to a mixing bowl and add the sautéed onions and the cheese. Whisk the egg whites to form stiff peaks, and fold in.

Spoon the chipa guasu mixture into 6 lightly greased 6-ounce ramekins and place on a baking sheet. When you have removed the ribs from the oven, turn the oven down to 350° and bake the chipa guasu until browned on top, I5 minutes. Remove the ramekins and serve with the short ribs.

YIELD: 6 SERVINGS

Skirt Steak with Chimichurri and Sweet Potato Fries

The family of our maitre d' at one of my restaurants, Ariel Lacayo, owns the Los Ranchos steakhouse in Managua, the capital of Nicaragua. One day, he explained to me how they had introduced churrasco *(a traditional Argentinian dish made with skirt steak) to the menu. At Los Ranchos, they used filet mignon instead, cut like skirt steak, and served it with chimichurri, an Argentinian-style steak sauce. This inspired me to create my own version of* churrasco.

Fresh Cilantro Marinade (page 11)
6 skirt steaks (about 8 ounces each), trimmed

Chimichurri

6 cloves garlic
3 bay leaves
2 jalapeño chiles, coarsely chopped, with seeds
1 1/2 tablespoons salt
1/2 cup finely minced fresh parsley
1/2 cup finely minced flat-leaf parsley
1/4 cup finely minced fresh oregano leaves
1/4 cup distilled white vinegar
1/3 cup extra virgin olive oil

Sweet Potato Fries

4 large sweet potatoes
3 cups canola oil, for deep-frying
Salt to taste

Combine the marinade and the skirt steaks in a large bowl. Cover, and let marinate in the refrigerator for about 3 hours. Turn the steaks over occasionally.

To prepare the chimichurri, mash the garlic, bay leaves, jalapeños, and salt with a mortar and pestle until a smooth paste is formed (or you can purée with a small amount of vinegar in a blender). Transfer to a mixing bowl and add the herbs. Whisk in the vinegar and olive oil until well mixed and set aside.

Preheat the oven to 400° and prepare the grill.

To prepare the fries, wrap each sweet potato in foil and place on a baking sheet. Bake in the oven for only 20 minutes; do not fully cook. Remove and let cool. Neatly cut the sweet potatoes into thin sticks, leaving the peel on.

In a deep fryer or saucepan, heat the oil to 350° and fry the sweet potato sticks until golden brown, 3 to 4 minutes. Season with salt.

Meanwhile, grill the steaks over a hot flame for about 3 minutes per side for medium, or to the desired doneness. Serve the steaks on top of the fries, and pour the chimichurri on top of the steaks.

YIELD: 6 SERVINGS

Opposite page: Skirt Steak with Chimichurri and Sweet Potato Fries

Grilled Loin of Lamb with Quinoa Salad and Papaya, Rosemary, and Garlic Mojo

Except for those parts of the Andean region where significant quantities of sheep are raised, lamb is not as widely popular or available as pork, beef, or chicken on most Latin American menus. I enjoy cooking with it, and in this recipe, I've paired it with a tropical mojo and quinoa salad. Quinoa was valued in pre-Columbian times for its nutritional qualities and because it grew in hardy conditions that no other crops (and especially corn) would tolerate. Although it's usually described as a grain, quinoa is actually the seed of a large herb.

4 boneless lamb loins, trimmed
Dry Adobo Rub (page 12)

Quinoa Salad

2 quarts water
$1\frac{1}{2}$ pounds quinoa, rinsed
$\frac{1}{2}$ cup chopped fresh parsley
$\frac{1}{4}$ cup chopped fresh oregano leaves
1 teaspoon minced garlic
3 tablespoons extra virgin olive oil
3 tablespoons sherry vinegar
Salt and pepper to taste

Papaya, Rosemary, and Garlic Mojo, refrigerated (page 44)

Thoroughly coat the lamb with the adobo rub. Transfer the lamb to a platter and let it sit in the refrigerator for 1 hour.

To prepare the salad, bring the water to a boil in a saucepan and add the quinoa. Cook over high heat for 6 minutes. Strain off the water and rinse the quinoa with cold water. Drain, transfer to a mixing bowl, and let cool for 10 minutes. Mix in the parsley, oregano, garlic, olive oil, vinegar, and salt and pepper and refrigerate until ready to use.

Preheat the grill.

Grill the lamb for 6 minutes per side for medium-rare. Serve with the mojo and quinoa salad.

YIELD: 4 SERVINGS

Opposite page: Grilled Loin of Lamb with Quinoa Salad and Papaya, Rosemary, and Garlic Mojo

Rabo Encendido
with Plantain-Ginger Flan

*Rabo encendido, which literally means "tail on fire," is hearty Latin fare. It's tradition-
ally a spicy oxtail stew, and here I've kept the oxtail whole and enhanced its robust
flavors with a cooling, sweet flan that can be used with many other dishes as well.
(Here again, the recipe will be made easier if you ask your butcher to cut the oxtail
for you.)*

Oxtail

4 pounds lean oxtails, trimmed of fat,
    and cut into 2 to 3-inch pieces
Seasoned Flour (page 8)
$^1/_2$ cup vegetable oil
1 onion, chopped
6 cloves garlic
3 carrots, chopped
5 stalks celery, chopped
1 teaspoon chopped fresh thyme leaves
2 bay leaves
1 tablespoon peppercorns
2 teaspoons crushed red pepper flakes
1 teaspoon ground cayenne pepper
3 tablespoons tomato paste
1 bottle (750 ml.) dry red wine
2 quarts water

Flan

2 semiripe plantains, peeled and
    sliced into 1-inch pieces
4 eggs, separated
1 tablespoon chopped gingerroot
$^1/_2$ cup milk
$^1/_2$ cup evaporated milk
1 teaspoon sugar
Salt and pepper to taste

1 cup Demi-Glace (page 10)
Perfect White Rice (page 8)
Garlic Plantain Chips (page 27)
6 chives, cut into 2-inch lengths

Preheat the oven to 400°.

Dredge the oxtail pieces in the seasoned flour. Heat the oil in a Dutch oven
or ovenproof casserole, and brown the
oxtail over high heat.

Add the remaining stew ingredients
and braise in the oven for $3^1/_2$ to 4 hours,
or until the meat flakes off the bone.

To prepare the flan, place the plantains in a saucepan and cover with water.
Bring to a boil, reduce the heat to
medium, and simmer for 10 minutes.
Drain the plantains and let cool. Transfer
to a blender and add the egg yolks, ginger, milk, and evaporated milk. Purée for
1 minute. Add the sugar, salt, and pepper, and blend for 5 seconds. Transfer
the mixture to a bowl.

Whisk the egg whites to form stiff
peaks, and fold into the plantain mixture. Pour into 6 lightly greased 6-ounce
ramekins and place in a water bath filled
with enough hot water to come halfway
up the sides of the ramekins. When the
oxtail has finished cooking, turn the oven
down to 350° and bake the flan for
20 minutes, or until firm in the middle.

Meanwhile, let the oxtail cool for
15 minutes. Transfer the oxtail to a large
bowl. Strain the liquid into a large
saucepan, discarding the vegetables. Reduce the liquid over high heat to $^3/_4$ cup,
or until it is thick enough to coat the
back of a spoon. Add the demi-glace and
continue to reduce for 15 minutes over
high heat.

Return the oxtail to the pan and coat
with the sauce. Cover the pan, reduce the
heat, and simmer for 10 minutes.

Turn the flan out of the ramekins,
running a knife around the inside edges
if necessary. Serve the oxtail with the
sauce, rice, and flan. Garnish the flan
with the plantain chips and sprinkle the
chives over the rice.

YIELD: 6 SERVINGS

Opposite page: Rabo Encendido with Plantain-Ginger Flan

DESSERTS & ICE CREAMS

Opposite page: Banana Tres Leches

LATIN DESSERTS ARE distinctly diverse. In many parts of South America, dessert is simply fresh fruit. In Puerto Rico or Mexico, on the other hand, it's likely to be a rich pudding or flan. In some Latin American countries, sweet dishes and pastries are consumed as a mid-morning or afternoon snack rather than an after-dinner dessert.

Latin desserts are very much influenced by Spanish traditions, and they tend to be filling and comforting if not verging on the decadent. Desserts are usually very sweet in countries like Cuba, no doubt because of the heavy local use of sugar, which is considered patriotic. Many Latin desserts are dairy based, perhaps because their effect is considered calming and a balance to the strong, spicy flavors that have been enjoyed earlier in the meal. Milk is also an inexpensive ingredient that's generally available throughout Latin America, whether fresh or in condensed or evaporated form.

Another common feature of Latin desserts is the use of tropical fruit. Traveling in South America, I was struck by the popularity of canned fruit in syrup—further evidence of the Latin sweet tooth. Poaching and preserving fruit are seen as practical means of keeping mango, papaya, guava, pineapple, and the like available throughout the year.

Flan is a universally popular dessert, and most Latin countries also have their own version of rice pudding. I prefer the loosely textured Cuban style; others are firmer and thicker.

My favorite desserts, though, are ice creams, which are popular in all Latin cuisines. I have also included some sorbet recipes in this chapter, although *granizados* or shaved ice is the more common style in most countries.

It just so happens that many of the desserts in this chapter need to set or chill overnight in the refrigerator. Bear this in mind when planning a meal.

Banana Tres Leches

Tres leches *is a classic Nicaraguan dessert, usually made with a white cake soaked with three different forms of* leches *or milks. This is one of the best-selling desserts at my restaurants. I like it because it is even easier to prepare than the Chocolate Tres Leches or Apple Tres Leches (recipes for them follow this one). Topped with Sweet Whipped Cream and vanilla meringue, this is a favorite for children too. When peaches are in season, you can substitute peach schnapps for the banana liqueur. Also, if you will be serving this to children, you may use artificial flavoring (found in the spice section of the supermarket) for the liqueurs. The meringue can be made a day in advance and stored in an airtight container.* Pictured on page 138.

Meringue

3 egg whites, at room temperature
$1/3$ cup granulated sugar
$1/8$ teaspoon pure vanilla extract
$3/4$ cup confectioners' sugar

Batter

5 eggs, at room temperature
I cup granulated sugar
$1/4$ cup water
I cup cake flour
I teaspoon baking powder
Pinch salt

Milk Topping

I can ($14^1/_2$ ounces) sweetened condensed milk
I can (12 ounces) evaporated milk
$1^1/_2$ cups heavy cream
$1/2$ cups banana liqueur

Sweet Whipped Cream

I cup heavy whipping cream
$1/4$ teaspoon pure vanilla extract
$1/4$ cup granulated sugar

2 bananas, peeled and sliced, for garnish
I cup stewed prunes, for garnish

Preheat the oven to 250°.

To make the meringue, beat the egg whites, granulated sugar, and vanilla extract until stiff peaks form. (Warming the bowl and beaters in warm water and drying carefully before using helps ensure high volume after beating.) Add the confectioners' sugar to the bowl and blend in quickly and thoroughly by hand. Transfer the meringue to a pastry bag and pipe strips of meringue onto a baking sheet. Place the pan in the preheated oven for about I hour, or until meringue is dry. Break the meringue into pieces and set aside.

Preheat the oven to 400°.

To make the batter, place the eggs in the mixing bowl of an electric mixer, add the sugar, and mix on high speed. Add the water, and continue beating until mixture is fluffy and pale yellow. Meanwhile, sift the flour, baking powder, and salt together and set aside. Remove the bowl from the mixer and add the dry ingredients. Add the flour mixture to the eggs as soon as they are ready and blend by hand thoroughly and quickly. (If this step is not done quickly enough, the eggs will lose their volume.)

Lightly grease a 13 by 9-inch cake pan. Pour the mixture into the prepared pan and tap firmly once or twice on the counter to remove any air bubbles. Immediately place the pan in the preheated oven. Bake for 10 to 13 minutes, or until a cake tester comes out clean when inserted in the middle. Remove the cake and let cool. While the cake is cooling, whisk together the milk topping ingredients. Using a toothpick, poke holes into the cake, pour the milk mixture over the top, and refrigerate.

In a well-chilled bowl using chilled beaters, beat the cream, vanilla extract, and sugar until stiff peaks form.

To assemble the cake, cut into serving pieces and place a scoop of whipped cream on top. Garnish with pieces of reserved meringue. Place slices of banana and a couple of the prunes around the plate for additional garnish.

YIELD: 12 SERVINGS

Chocolate Tres Leches

This recipe was perfected by Alicia LaRosa, a talented former pastry chef of mine. I liked her recipe so much I kept it on the menu at Yuca and it's still on their menu! The mousse, which can also be made as a dessert all on its own, should be made a day ahead.

Chocolate Mousse

7 ounces semi-sweet chocolate, chopped

$1/4$ cup heavy cream

6 egg yolks

$1/4$ cup sugar

1 tablespoon Grand Marnier or
  Cointreau (optional)

$1^1/_2$ cups heavy cream, whipped

Cake

1 cup all-purpose flour

$1/4$ cup cocoa powder

1 teaspoon baking powder

$1/2$ teaspoon salt

5 eggs, at room temperature

1 cup sugar

$1/3$ cup water

2 teaspoons pure vanilla extract

Tres Leches

1 can (12 ounces) evaporated milk

1 can ($14^1/_2$ ounces) condensed milk

$1^1/_2$ cups heavy cream

2 tablespoons Hershey's chocolate syrup

Meringue

1 cup confectioners' sugar

$1/4$ cup cocoa powder

5 egg whites, at room temperature

$1/2$ cup granulated sugar

To prepare the mousse, in a double boiler, melt the chocolate in the cream. Remove from the heat and let cool slightly.

With an electric mixer on high speed, beat the egg yolks and sugar in a mixing bowl until pale yellow and doubled in volume (or whisk vigorously over a water bath or double boiler until you achieve the same results).

Quickly beat in the melted chocolate mixture, all at once. Add the liqueur, if desired. Gently fold in the whipped cream until thoroughly incorporated. Place in the refrigerator and chill overnight.

The next day, preheat the oven to 400°.

To prepare the cake, sift the flour, cocoa powder, baking powder, and salt into a mixing bowl and set aside. In another mixing bowl, beat the eggs and sugar with an electric mixer on high speed for about 2 minutes. With the mixer running, add the water and vanilla all at once and continue beating until the mixture is fluffy, pale yellow, and doubled in volume, about 10 minutes.

Turn off the mixer and quickly fold in the reserved dry ingredients. (If you take too long, the eggs will drop in volume.) Pour the cake batter into a lightly buttered 13 by 9-inch cake pan and firmly tap once or twice to remove any air bubbles.

Transfer the pan immediately to the oven and bake until a toothpick inserted comes out clean, about 10 minutes. Remove from the oven and let cool.

Meanwhile, whisk all of the tres leches ingredients together in a large mixing bowl until well blended.

Run a knife around the edges of the cake pan and poke holes in the entire surface of the cake with a toothpick. Pour the milk mixture over the cake, 1 cup at a time, until the cake can't absorb any more liquid. Cover and reserve in the refrigerator. Use any excess milk mixture for shakes.

Reheat the oven to 200°.

To prepare the meringue, sift the confectioners' sugar and cocoa together into a mixing bowl and set aside. In a mixing bowl, beat the egg whites and sugar with an electric mixer until they form stiff peaks. Add the cocoa mixture all at once, and fold in until thoroughly incorporated.

Transfer the meringue to a pastry bag fitted with a plain tip. Pipe spirals of meringue onto parchment paper and sprinkle with the granulated sugar. Place in the oven for 1 hour, or until dry. (You can do this up to 3 days in advance and store the strips in an airtight container.) Remove from the oven and set aside.

To serve, cut the cake into pieces. Spread the refrigerated mousse on the cake and garnish each serving with a meringue spiral.

YIELD: 12 TO 15 SERVINGS

Opposite page: Chocolate Tres Leches

Apple Tres Leches Americana

This dessert uses the same basic concept as the Chocolate Tres Leches recipe (page 142), but the results are very different because the apples are actually in the cake.

My former pastry chef, Trish, created this dessert the first time I cooked for the venerable Julia Child. It seemed perfect because it represented a harmony of our two cultures; on the one hand, its origins were Latin (like me), but the twist of using apples seemed all-American (like Trish). I'll never forget how excited Trish was to meet her long-time inspiration and mentor. Julia loved her meal and was gracious as always, making it a night we'll never forget.

In this recipe, I suggest that you peel and slice the apples right after the poaching liquid has been prepared to prevent them from turning brown.

Poached Apples

1^1/$_2$ quarts water
2^1/$_4$ cups sugar
2 star anise
2 whole cloves
1 vanilla bean, halved lengthwise
1 stick cinnamon
6 to 8 strips lemon zest
   (about 1 inch long)
Juice of 2 lemons
6 Granny Smith apples

Meringue

^{1}/$_2$ cup water
1 cup light corn syrup
1^1/$_2$ cups sugar
^{1}/$_2$ teaspoon cinnamon extract
3 egg whites, at room temperature

Cake

1 cup all-purpose flour
1 teaspoon baking powder
Pinch salt
5 eggs, at room temperature
1 cup sugar
^{1}/$_4$ cup water

Tres Leches

1 can (14^1/$_2$ ounces) condensed milk
1 can (12 ounces) evaporated milk
1^1/$_2$ cups heavy cream
^{1}/$_2$ cup (or to taste) apple schnapps

^{1}/$_4$ cup sugar
12 sticks cinnamon, for garnish

To prepare the poached apples, combine the water, sugar, star anise, cloves, vanilla bean, cinnamon stick, lemon zest, and lemon juice in a large saucepan and bring to a boil. Stir constantly until the sugar is dissolved, then reduce the heat to low and let simmer. Quickly peel, seed, and cut each apple into 3 wedges. (You should have 18 pieces about 2^1/$_2$ inches in diameter.) Add the wedges to the pan. Reduce the heat even lower and simmer until the apples are barely soft, about 10 minutes.

Remove the cooked apples from the liquid with a slotted spoon, discarding the poaching mixture, and let cool. Dice 6 of the apple slices and reserve for the cake. Set the remaining 12 slices aside for the garnish.

To prepare the meringue, combine the water, corn syrup, and sugar together in a heavy-bottomed saucepan. Stirring constantly, bring to a boil over medium heat. Continue stirring and cook until a small amount dropped into a glass of water spins a thread (about 227°), 30 minutes.

Stir in the cinnamon extract, being careful not to breathe in the vapors. Remove the pan from the heat.

In a mixing bowl, beat the egg whites with an electric mixer on high speed until they form stiff peaks. Reduce the speed to medium-low and add the sugar-syrup mixture in a slow, steady stream until incorporated. Let cool, then cover and reserve in the refrigerator.

Preheat the oven to 400°. Lightly grease a 13 by 9-inch cake pan.

To prepare the cake, sift the flour, baking powder, and salt into a mixing bowl and set aside. In another bowl, beat the eggs and sugar with an electric mixer on high speed for about 2 minutes. With the mixer running, add the water all at once and continue beating until the mixture is fluffy, pale yellow, and doubled in volume, about 10 minutes.

Turn off the mixer and quickly fold in the reserved dry ingredients. (If you take too long, the eggs will drop in volume.) Pour the cake batter into the prepared pan and firmly tap once or twice to remove any air bubbles. Sprinkle the reserved diced apple on top of the batter.

Immediately transfer the pan to the oven and bake until a toothpick inserted comes out clean, 10 to 15 minutes. Remove from the oven and let cool.

Meanwhile, whisk all of the milk mixture ingredients together in a large mixing bowl until well blended.

Poke holes in the entire surface of cake with a toothpick. Pour the milk mixture over the cake, 1 cup at a time, until the cake can't absorb any more liquid. Cover and reserve in the refrigerator.

To prepare the apple garnish, make cuts almost to the ends of the remaining apple wedges to create fans and place on a baking sheet. Sprinkle the apples with the $\frac{1}{4}$ cup of sugar and caramelize the sugar with a hand-held propane torch until nicely browned (or place under the broiler).

To serve, cut the chilled cake into 12 slices. Place each slice onto a serving plate and top with a dollop of meringue. Place an apple fan on top of the meringue and garnish with a cinnamon stick.

YIELD: 12 SERVINGS

Coco Cabana

This coconut cream pudding is served with tropical flair—inside a coconut shell. Once, we made a thousand of these for a charity event to benefit SOS (Save Our Strength), a Washington, DC–based organization committed to feeding the hungry. This version of coconut pudding will make converts out of those who never liked coconut before.

1 can Coco Lopez

$2\frac{1}{2}$ cups heavy cream

2 eggs

5 egg yolks

1 cup shredded coconut

4 coconuts, halved

$\frac{1}{4}$ cup sugar

Place the Coco Lopez in a saucepan over a double boiler and reduce by half over medium-high heat, stirring constantly, about 15 to 20 minutes. Stir in the cream and return to a boil for 1 minute. Remove from the heat.

Meanwhile, in a mixing bowl, beat the eggs and egg yolks with an electric mixer at high speed until the mixture is fluffy and light yellow, about 10 minutes. Reduce the speed to low, and add the hot cream mixture in a slow, fine stream, whisking constantly. (If you add it too fast, the eggs will curdle.) Add the shredded coconut and mix thoroughly.

Preheat the oven to 300°.

Pour the mixture into an ovenproof baking dish. Place in a water bath and add enough hot water to come halfway up the sides of the baking dish. Bake for 30 minutes.

Remove the baking dish from the oven, let cool slightly, and then refrigerate overnight.

To serve, spoon the chilled mixture into the coconut halves, sprinkle the sugar on top, and caramelize with a hand-held propane torch (or under the broiler).

YIELD: 8 SERVINGS

Rice Pudding in Almond Baskets

This is a very traditional Latin dessert, but the presentation is pure Nuevo Latino. To mold the baskets, I recommend using some 14-ounce cans such as cans of condensed milk. (It's fine if they're unopened.) Or, you can use the curved bottom of a cereal bowl. This recipe makes more baskets than you will need for the rice pudding, but the recipe won't work in smaller quantities. Store the extra baskets in an airtight container for a day or two, and use for ice cream, sorbets, or fruit salad.

Almond Baskets

1 cup plus 1 tablespoon butter, softened
2 tablespoons sugar
6 egg whites, in separate containers
$1/2$ cup plus 1 tablespoon all-purpose flour
6 ounces thinly sliced almonds

Rice Pudding

7 ounces Valencia short-grain rice
$3^1/_2$ cups water
$1/2$ teaspoon salt
1 stick cinnamon
$1/2$ cup plus 2 tablespoons heavy cream
$1/2$ cup plus 2 tablespoons evaporated milk
$1/2$ cup condensed milk
$3/4$ cup sugar
$1/4$ cup raisins (optional)

Garnish

16 sticks cinnamon
$1/4$ cup ground cinammon

To prepare the baskets, place the butter and sugar together in a food processor and cream until well blended. With the machine running, add the egg whites, one at a time, until incorporated. Add the flour and almonds all at once and blend together well. Transfer the batter to a mixing bowl, cover, and refrigerate for 7 to 8 hours.

Preheat the oven to 400°.

Line 2 baking sheets with parchment paper. Pour about $1/4$ cup of the batter onto the parchment paper and spread thinly into a 7-inch circle. Repeat until you have used half of the batter and there are about 8 circles.

Bake in the oven until golden brown, about 10 minutes, watching carefully so that the baskets don't get too brown. Remove the baking sheets from the oven and let cool for about 3 minutes until the cookies are still warm but not hot.

Make slashes in the parchment paper around each cookie and lift the parchment paper and warm cookies off the baking sheet. Mold them around the end of some cans (the edges will droop over automatically), and let cool completely.

When cool, carefully remove the molded baskets from the cans, peel off the paper, and set aside.

Repeat by pouring the remaining batter on relined baking sheets and making the baskets as above. (Cooking in 2 batches reduces the risk of the cookies hardening before you can mold them.)

To prepare the pudding, place the rice and water in a saucepan. Bring to a boil, reduce the heat to medium, and cook for 20 minutes. Add the salt and cinnamon. Stirring constantly, pour in the cream about 2 tablespoons at a time so that the mixture does not cool down too much.

Add the evaporated milk in 2-tablespoon increments, stirring constantly until mixed in. Repeat with the condensed milk, and continue cooking the mixture for 15 minutes.

Stir in the sugar and cook for another 10 minutes. Remove from the heat, let cool, and add the raisins. The pudding will thicken as it cools. Chill in the refrigerator overnight.

To serve, spoon the chilled pudding into each of the baskets. Garnish with 2 cinnamon sticks and a sprinkle of ground cinnamon.

YIELD: 8 SERVINGS

Opposite page: Rice Pudding in Almond Baskets

Pumpkin Flan
with Gingersnap Crust

This flan is my variation of a classic Cuban dessert that's usually made with calabaza (also known as West Indian pumpkin). I've added a crunchy gingersnap crust, and the overall effect is like a cheesecake with a crispy crust. Use canned pumpkin if calabaza is unavailable.

Flan

8 ounces calabaza or pumpkin, peeled, seeded, and cut into $1/2$-inch dice
I can ($14^1/_2$ ounces) condensed milk
I can (12 ounces) evaporated milk
8 eggs
3 tablespoons sugar

Caramel

I cup sugar

Crust

I pound gingersnap cookies
$1/_2$ cup melted butter

To prepare the flan, bring a saucepan of water to a boil. Add the calabaza and cook until tender, about 30 minutes. Drain the calabaza and let cool. Transfer to a food processor, add the condensed and evaporated milk, eggs, and the 3 tablespoons of sugar and purée until smooth. Set aside.

Preheat the oven to 375°.

To make the caramel, place the cup of sugar in a heavy-bottomed saucepan and cook, stirring constantly, over medium heat until the sugar is a light amber color, about 20 minutes. Pour the caramel into a 9 by 4-inch loaf pan or into 6 individual 8-ounce ramekins or molds. Pour the reserved flan mixture on top of the caramel and place in a water bath. Bake for 15 minutes.

Reduce the oven temperature to 350°, and bake until set (a knife inserted will come out clean), about 30 minutes. Remove from the oven and let cool completely.

To prepare the crust, place the cookies and butter in a food processor and process until well blended. Pack the crust mixture on top of the cooled flan, and transfer to the refrigerator to chill overnight.

To serve, run a knife around the inside edges of the loaf pan or molds and invert onto a serving platter or individual plates.

YIELD: 6 SERVINGS

Chocolate-Rum Flan

Flan is a straightforward dessert to make, and it's a great medium for other flavors. I've always loved chocolate flan, but in this recipe, you can substitute a fruit flavor for the chocolate or an orange liqueur for the rum. The most important thing to remember is to not overcook it.

Flan

1 can (14$\frac{1}{2}$ ounces) condensed milk
1 can (12 ounces) evaporated milk
2 eggs
6 egg yolks
$\frac{1}{4}$ cup Hershey's chocolate syrup
2 tablespoons dark rum

Caramel

1 cup sugar

Place the condensed and evaporated milk, eggs and egg yolks, chocolate, and rum in a food processor or blender and mix together thoroughly.

Preheat the oven to 375°.

To make the caramel, place the sugar in a heavy-bottomed saucepan and cook over medium heat, stirring constantly, until the sugar is a light amber color, about 20 minutes. Pour the caramel into 6 individual 8-ounce ramekins or molds, or a 9 by 4-inch loaf pan.

Pour the flan mixture into the ramekins or molds on top of the caramel. Place in a water bath and bake uncovered in the oven for 15 minutes. Reduce the heat to 350° and continue baking until set, when a knife inserted comes out clean, about 30 minutes. Remove from the oven and let cool completely.

To serve, run a knife around the inside edges of the ramekins or molds and invert the flans onto a serving platter or individual plates.

YIELD: 6 SERVINGS

Flan and Figs

Port wine and anise are two flavors that make a good pair. This recipe was developed after I discovered that the deep color of the port made a somewhat gray-colored flan. To lighten the color, I added white wine. The result was wonderful, and the figs contribute and interesting texture.

Flan

4 cups milk
3 star anise
$\frac{3}{4}$ cup sugar
7 eggs

Caramel

1$\frac{1}{2}$ cups sugar
Pepper to taste

Figs

1 cup white wine
$\frac{1}{2}$ cup Myer's dark rum
1 stick cinnamon
30 dried figs

To prepare the flan, heat the milk and star anise in a saucepan until barely simmering. Over low heat, keep to just under a simmer for about 30 minutes, to infuse. Turn off the heat, let cool, and remove the star anise.

Whisk the sugar and eggs into the cooled milk, and set the flan mixture aside.

Preheat the oven to 300°.

To prepare the caramel, place the sugar in a heavy-bottomed saucepan and cook, stirring constantly, over medium heat until the sugar is a light amber color, about 20 minutes. Sprinkle some pepper into 10 individual 6-ounce ramekins or molds, and add the caramel.

Pour the flan mixture into the ramekins, on top of the caramel. Place in a water bath, cover with foil, and bake in the oven for 1$\frac{3}{4}$ hours.

Meanwhile, prepare the figs. Place the wine, rum, and cinnamon stick in a saucepan and bring to a low boil. Add the figs, return to a low boil, and cook for 5 minutes. Remove the pan from the heat and let cool. Refrigerate the figs overnight.

When the flans are cooked, remove them from the oven and let cool. Chill in the refrigerator overnight.

To serve, run a knife around the inside edges of the ramekins or molds and invert the flans onto a serving platter or individual plates. Garnish with 3 figs per serving and some of the fig liquid.

YIELD: 10 SERVINGS

Brazo Park Avenue with Banana Mousse

The name of this dessert is a play on words. Brazo gitano, *literally "gypsy's arm," is a classical Cuban dessert that's like a jelly roll stuffed with* natilla, *or white custard. I named my version after the New York address of one of my restaurants. Instead of the traditional custard filling, I use a banana mousse. The recipe is somewhat involved, but it's an impressive dessert that's well worth the effort.*

Filling

3 small ripe bananas, well mashed
2 tablespoons freshly squeezed lemon juice
1 cup confectioners' sugar
1½ teaspoons unflavored gelatin
2 tablespoons cold water
¼ cup boiling water
1 cup heavy cream, whipped

Cake

1 cup all-purpose flour
3 tablespoons cocoa powder
1 teaspoon baking powder
Pinch salt
6 eggs, at room temperature
1 cup sugar
1 teaspoon pure vanilla extract
½ cup water, at room temperature

Chocolate Coating

6 ounces semi-sweet chocolate, chopped
2 tablespoons butter
3 tablespoons milk
2 tablespoons light corn syrup

Chocolate Mousse (page 142)
6 dried banana chips

To prepare the filling, combine the mashed bananas and lemon juice in a mixing bowl and mix well. Sift the confectioners' sugar on top of the bananas and set aside.

In a separate mixing bowl, dissolve the gelatin in the cold water. Stir in the boiling water and let cool for 1 or 2 minutes before adding to the bananas. Quickly fold the whipped cream into the mixture and refrigerate for about 1 hour, to allow it to firm up.

Preheat the oven to 400°.

To prepare the cake, sift the flour, cocoa powder, baking powder, and salt into a mixing bowl, and set aside. In another bowl, beat the eggs, sugar, and vanilla with an electric mixer on high speed for about 5 minutes. With the mixer running, slowly add the water, and continue beating until the mixture turns fluffy and pale yellow, about 5 to 10 minutes.

Quickly and evenly, fold the dry ingredients into the egg mixture. (If you take too long, the eggs will drop in volume.) Pour the cake batter into a lightly buttered jelly-roll pan lined with parchment paper, and spread gently and quickly to the edges. Tap the pan firmly once or twice to remove any air bubbles.

Transfer the pan immediately to the oven and bake until the center of the cake springs back when touched, 10 minutes. Remove the pan from the oven and let cool slightly for 1 or 2 minutes.

Invert the pan onto a large sheet of parchment paper and peel off the top sheet of parchment paper (that was in-

side the pan). Roll up the wide side of the cake with the paper (that is, rolling both up), and twist the paper ends closed. Set aside for a few minutes.

Unroll the cake and parchment paper on a flat work surface. Spread out the refrigerated filling to within 1 inch of the edges of the cake, and place the cake in the refrigerator for 10 minutes. Then carefully re-roll the cake, this time wrapping the parchment paper around the outside of the cake. Reserve in the refrigerator while preparing the coating.

Place the chocolate and butter in the top of a double boiler and heat until melted. Remove the pot from the heat and stir in the milk and corn syrup.

Take a large enough piece of firm cardboard (at least 11 by 5 inches) to sit the cake on, and cover with aluminum foil. Remove the roll from the refrigerator, take off the parchment paper, and place the cake on the foil, seam-side down. Rotate slightly to just expose the seam side of the cake and drizzle with about half of the coating. Spread the coating smoothly and evenly with a spatula, making sure that the seam side of the roll is covered. Place the roll, with the cardboard and foil base, in the refrigerator and let it set for about 15 minutes.

Remove the roll from the refrigerator and repeat the coating process on the other side, so that the whole cake is covered. Any leftover coating can be used to cover any cracks or breaks. To set once more, refrigerate for 15 minutes. Dot the top with the Chocolate Mousse and set the banana chips in the mousse. Cut the roll in slices and serve.

YIELD: 12 TO 16 SERVINGS

Opposite page: Brazo Park Avenue with Banana Mousse

Papaya-Cream Cheese Terrine

I've worked with a few pastry chefs in my time, but no one can match the talent of Marta Browstein when it comes to fruit terrines. She originally created this recipe using guavas. I've simply adapted it for one of my favorite fruits, the papaya. This is the ultimate recipe for cheese and fruit lovers. It's also pretty to look at.

1 papaya, peeled, seeded, and very
   thinly sliced
$1/2$ teaspoon grated lemon zest
$1/2$ teaspoon grated orange zest
$1/4$ cup plus 2 tablespoons sugar
1 cup sour cream
1 cup cream cheese
2 teaspoons unflavored gelatin
1 tablespoon cold water
2 tablespoons boiling water
$1/2$ cup passion fruit juice
1 cup heavy cream, whipped

Mango Water

1 cup mango juice (about 2 mangoes)
$1/4$ cup sugar
$1/2$ cup water
$1/4$ slivered lime zest

Place the papaya, lemon and orange zest, and $1/4$ cup of the sugar in a mixing bowl and gently toss. In a separate mixing bowl, cream the remaining 2 tablespoons of sugar with the sour cream and cream cheese until smooth.

In another mixing bowl, dissolve the gelatin in the cold water. Stir in the boiling water to dissolve thoroughly, and then stir in the passion fruit juice. Fold into the cream cheese mixture, and then fold in the whipped cream until incorporated.

To assemble the terrine, drain the papaya and lay out on paper towels. Place a thin layer (about $1/8$ inch) of the cream cheese mixture in the bottom of a lightly oiled loaf pan and spread out evenly. Place a layer of the papaya slices on top of the cream cheese, and continue layering alternately, finishing with the cream cheese mixture. Place in the refrigerator overnight to completely set.

To prepare the mango water, combine the mango juice, sugar, and water in a saucepan. Bring to a boil, reduce the heat to medium-low, and simmer for about 15 minutes, stirring constantly. Strain, then transfer to a bowl, add the lime zest, and chill.

To serve, run a knife around the inside edge of the pan and gently and quickly turn over onto a serving platter. Slice the terrine with a sharp knife, and lay a slice of it in the center of each serving plate. Spoon the mango water around the edge of each slice.

YIELD: 8 TO 10 SERVINGS

Opposite page: Papaya–Cream Cheese Terrine

Apple Buñuelos

Buñuelos are deep-fried pastries sprinkled with sugar. They are similar to the beignets of New Orleans, and most Latin American countries have their own version. These buñuelos are not entirely traditional, but I don't think you'll care, once you experience their soft texture and fruit flavor. This recipe needs to be started the night before it's served.

2 cups butter
6 Granny Smith apples, peeled, cored, and chopped
1 stick cinnamon
$\frac{1}{2}$ tablespoon unflavored gelatin
$1\frac{1}{2}$ tablespoons cold water
$\frac{1}{4}$ cup boiling water
3 egg yolks
1 tablespoon sour cream
1 cup all-purpose flour
2 eggs, lightly beaten

1 cup vegetable oil, for frying
1 cup confectioners' sugar
1 cup heavy cream, whipped

Melt the butter in a saucepan. Add the apples and cinnamon stick, and bring to a gentle simmer. Cook for 15 minutes, stirring occasionally, until the apples are tender.

Meanwhile, in a mixing bowl, dissolve the gelatin in the cold water. Stir in the boiling water to dissolve thoroughly. In a separate mixing bowl, gently beat the egg yolks and sour cream together. Stir in the gelatin mixture.

When the apples are tender, fold into the gelatin mixture. Transfer to a clean bowl, let cool, and refrigerate overnight.

Remove the apple mixture from the refrigerator and make 35 to 40 small balls using a melon baller or mini ice cream scoop. Place the flour in a bowl, roll the balls in the flour, and refrigerate again for 10 to 15 minutes.

When ready to serve, heat the vegetable oil to 350° in a large pan or skillet. Roll the balls once more in the flour, then in the beaten egg. Roll in the flour a final time and fry in the hot oil until golden brown, about 3 minutes, turning to fry on all sides.

Drain on paper towels, sprinkle with confectioners' sugar, and serve immediately with whipped cream.

**YIELD: 6 TO 8 SERVINGS
(35 TO 40 1-INCH BALLS)**

Poached Guava Shells

You can find canned guava shells in syrup in Latin markets, but the homemade version always tastes best. This is the traditional way of eating guavas for dessert with cheese. I suggest serving them with vanilla ice cream (page 158) and honey graham crackers. For the most colorful results, use the reddest guavas you can find. The shells can be stored in the refrigerator for up to 1 week.

6 cups water

6 cups sugar

15 firm guavas, peeled, halved, and seeded

Place the water and sugar in a large saucepan. Cook over medium heat, stirring occasionally, until the sugar dissolves.

Place the guava "shells" in the saucepan and lower the heat. Simmer, stirring occasionally, until tender, about 30 minutes.

Serve with ice cream or cream cheese.

YIELD: 15 SERVINGS

Guava-Cream Cheese Turnovers

Guava and cream cheese is a classic combination for Cuban desserts, and this is the recipe my grandmother used to make. She used margarine to keep the texture just right, and I'm not about to mess with family tradition! Guava paste is available in Latin markets, but orange marmalade makes a nice alternative.

1 cup margarine, softened

8 ounces cream cheese, softened

Pinch salt

2 cups all-purpose flour

8 ounces guava paste, cut into about 20 1/4-inch-thick slices, or 5 tablespoons orange marmalade

Place the margarine and cream cheese in a mixing bowl and cream until well blended. Add the salt and flour all at once, and mix well. Form into a dough, cover tightly with plastic wrap, and refrigerate for 15 minutes.

Preheat the oven to 375°.

Cut the dough in half, and working quickly, roll out the first half on a floured work surface to a thickness of about 1/8 inch. Cut this half of the dough into about ten 3-inch squares.

Place a slice of the guava paste (or, alternatively, about 3/4 teaspoon of marmalade) on each square. Fold two of the opposite corners of the dough over to meet in the middle, and seal with a pinch, turnover-style. Repeat for the other half of the dough, or freeze it and use it later.

Place the turnovers on a baking sheet and bake until golden brown, 15 minutes. Remove the turnovers from the oven and let cool on paper towels. Serve with vanilla ice cream, if desired.

YIELD: 10 SERVINGS (20 TURNOVERS)

Apple Sorbet

This is a light, refreshing dessert that goes well with Apple Buñuelos (page 154). I use only Granny Smith apples for this recipe, because they produce the freshest-tasting sorbet.

1/2 cup sugar

1 cup water

1/2 cup light corn syrup

2 drops green food coloring (optional)

Juice of 2 lemons

15 Granny Smith apples, peeled, cored, and cut into 1-inch cubes

2 Granny Smith apples, unpeeled and thinly sliced, for garnish

Combine the sugar and water together in a heavy-bottomed saucepan and bring to a strong boil, without stirring. Remove from the heat and let cool. Transfer to a mixing bowl, add the corn syrup, food coloring, and lemon juice, and mix well.

Juice the apple cubes in a juice extractor and stir the juice into the sugar mixture. Pour into the container of an ice cream machine and freeze according to the manufacturer's directions. Garnish with the apple slices.

YIELD: 1 QUART

Coconut Ice Milk

This rich-tasting dessert is a must for coconut lovers. In South America, coconut ice is a popular and soothing refreshment.

2 cups milk

1 cup sugar

1 can (14 ounces) unsweetened coconut milk

2 tablespoons dark rum

Bring the milk and sugar to a boil in a heavy-bottomed saucepan, stirring occasionally. Remove from the heat and let cool.

Stir in the coconut milk and rum, and transfer to an ice cream machine. Freeze according to the manufacturer's directions.

YIELD: 1¹/₄ QUARTS

Opposite page: Apple Sorbet

Spice Cake Ice Cream

Carrot cake works best for this flavorful recipe, but you can use another cake with a similar consistency, or lady fingers. When removing the zest, use a vegetable peeler or knife, not a zester, so that it can be removed in large sections.

1¾ cups milk
1¼ cups heavy cream
Zest of 1 lemon
Zest of 1 orange
1 vanilla bean, split lengthwise and scraped
2 whole cloves
1 stick cinnamon
2 star anise
Pinch freshly grated nutmeg
Pinch pepper
10 tablespoons sugar
¼ cup water
6 egg yolks
1 slice store-bought carrot cake
    (4 to 5 ounces), frosting removed

Heat the milk, cream, zest, vanilla bean, cloves, cinnamon, anise, nutmeg, and pepper in a heavy-bottomed saucepan over medium heat. Meanwhile, heat 6 tablespoons of the sugar and the water in a separate saucepan over medium-high heat, stirring only when it turns a golden color.

When the milk mixture reaches a boil, quickly stir in the caramel. (Take care, because the milk will bubble profusely.) Continue to stir, and reduce the heat to very low.

Whisk together the egg yolks and remaining 4 tablespoons of sugar in a mixing bowl. Remove the milk mixture from the heat and strain. Pour this mixture slowly into the egg yolks to temper, whisking vigorously. (If you add it too fast, the eggs will curdle.) Place the mixture in a clean saucepan and cook over medium heat, stirring continuously, until the mixture thickens, about 10 minutes. Remove the pan from the heat.

Crumble the carrot cake into a large mixing bowl and pour in the custard. Mix well, chill, and then pour into an ice cream machine and freeze according to the manufacturer's directions.

YIELD: 1 QUART

Vanilla Ice Cream

If you're one of those many people who love vanilla ice cream, I suggest doubling this recipe so that you'll always have some on hand. The beauty of vanilla ice cream is that it's so versatile—it goes well with any fruit, or with just a splash of liqueur on top.

4 cups half-and-half
2 vanilla beans, split lengthwise
    and scraped
¾ cup sugar
8 egg yolks

Bring the half-and-half, vanilla beans, and ½ cup of the sugar to a boil in a heavy-bottomed saucepan, stirring occasionally. Reduce the heat to very low and barely simmer for 15 minutes, stirring occasionally.

Meanwhile, set up an ice-water bath with a stainless-steel bowl placed over it to chill.

In a separate bowl, whisk together the egg yolks and remaining ¼ cup of sugar. Return the half-and-half mixture to a low boil and slowly pour about one third of this mixture into the egg yolks to temper, whisking vigorously. (If you add it too fast, the eggs will curdle.)

Remove the remaining half-and-half mixture from the heat and slowly pour the tempered egg yolk mixture back into the pan, continuing to whisk vigorously. Transfer immediately into the chilled bowl over the ice-water bath and let cool, stirring occasionally.

When cool, strain into a bowl and transfer to an ice cream machine. Freeze according to the manufacturer's directions.

YIELD: 1¼ QUARTS

Cafe con Leche Ice Cream

This ice cream is one tasty Nuevo Latino dessert. Coffee ice cream has been around for a long time, but this creamy version tastes just like the strong cafe con leche. They say Latin mothers occasionally slip some cafe con leche into their baby's bottles, which might explain why most of the Latins I know are big coffee drinkers! Trust me, this dessert will convert those few who claim they don't enjoy coffee ice cream.

3 cups milk

1 cup heavy cream

1 cup plus 1 tablespoon sugar

$^{1}/_{2}$ cup freshly brewed, strong espresso coffee, chilled

1 tablespoon dried instant coffee

8 egg yolks

Bring the milk, cream, and $^{3}/_{4}$ cup of the sugar to a boil in a heavy-bottomed saucepan, stirring occasionally. Reduce the heat to very low and barely simmer for 15 minutes, stirring occasionally. Then add the espresso and stir in the instant coffee until dissolved.

Meanwhile, set up an ice-water bath with a stainless-steel bowl placed over it to chill.

In a separate bowl, whisk together the egg yolks and the remaining sugar. Return the milk and coffee mixture to a low boil and slowly pour about one third of this mixture into the egg yolks to temper, whisking vigorously. (If you add it too fast, the eggs will curdle.)

Remove the remaining milk mixture from the heat and slowly pour in the tempered egg yolk mixture back into the pan, continuing to whisk vigorously. Transfer immediately into the chilled bowl over the ice-water bath and let cool, stirring occasionally.

When cool, strain the mixture into a bowl and transfer to an ice cream machine. Freeze according to the manufacturer's directions.

YIELD: 1$^{1}/_{2}$ QUARTS

Guava-Cream Cheese Ice Cream

This may not be a traditional ice cream, but the combination of guava and ice cream is a Cuban favorite, and their beautiful flavors stand on their own. This is a quick and easy recipe that's ideal for the ice cream novice.

4 ounces cream cheese, softened

8 ounces ricotta cheese

$^{1}/_{2}$ cup light corn syrup

1 cup frozen guava purée, defrosted

Juice of 2 limes

Place the cream cheese, ricotta cheese, and corn syrup in a blender, and purée until very smooth. Add the guava purée and lime juice and blend well.

Transfer to an ice cream machine and freeze according to the manufacturer's directions.

YIELD: $^{3}/_{4}$ QUART

The Smokeless Macanudo

This recipe was developed by my first pastry chef at Patria, and we prepared 1,500 of these cigars for a single event—the Great American Smokeout, held in New York City. This is an opportunity for cigar smokers to enjoy a night out, with several fine restaurants preparing special dishes. Needless to say, our cigar dessert was the hit of the night!

Our restaurant version comes complete with an edible matchbook and edible matches, but the recipe for the matchbook is so complicated that I'm not going to put you through it. We sell about seventy of these desserts a night at the restaurant, so if you want to see the finished assembled dish, we'll have one waiting for you at my restaurant.

Cake

$^2/_3$ cup all-purpose flour

$^1/_4$ cup cocoa powder

$^1/_2$ teaspoon baking powder

$^1/_4$ teaspoon salt

4 eggs, at room temperature

$^1/_2$ cup sugar

I teaspoon pure vanilla extract

$^1/_4$ cup water

5 tablespoons melted butter

Filling

$4^1/_2$ cups heavy cream

$12^1/_2$ ounces semi-sweet chocolate, melted and cooled slightly

Coating

$4^1/_2$ ounces semi-sweet chocolate, melted

72 fresh mint leaves
washed and patted dry

I cup cocoa powder

$^1/_2$ cup confectioners' sugar

$^1/_2$ tablespoon ground cinnamon

I cup confectioners' sugar

$^1/_2$ cup cocoa powder

Spice Cake Ice Cream (page 158)

Preheat the oven to 400°. Grease a jelly-roll pan and line it with parchment paper.

Sift the flour, cocoa powder, baking powder, and salt into a mixing bowl. In another bowl, beat the eggs and sugar with an electric mixer on high speed. Add the vanilla and water all at once and continue beating until the mixture triples in volume.

Working quickly so that you don't lose too much volume, turn off the mixer, add the flour mixture all at once, and fold in to form a batter.

Place the butter in a separate mixing bowl, add about I cup of the batter, and blend well. Add this to the remaining batter and blend in quickly.

Pour the batter into the prepared jelly-roll pan. Bake in the oven for 10 minutes. Remove the pan and let cool.

To prepare the filling, chill a stainless-steel bowl and a whisk. Beat the cream in the chilled bowl until whipped. Fold in the melted chocolate by hand. The mixture will be somewhat crumbly.

Cut the long side of the cooled cake in half. Spread $^3/_4$ to I cup of the chocolate-cream mixture on one side of the cake, and top with the other half of the cake, forming a sandwich. Neatly trim all the edges of the cake.

Make one cigar at a time. Lay out an 8-inch square of plastic wrap on a work surface. Cut the cake into $^5/_8$-inch-wide strips and place in the center of the plastic wrap. Using about 2 to $2^1/_2$ tablespoons of the filling, place small blobs along each strip of cake and at both ends. Carefully roll up the plastic wrap around the cake and filling; twist the ends to close.

Using the warmth of your hands and fingers, gently squeeze and mold the filling around the cake to form a cigar-shaped cylinder. (It becomes easier after the first one or two.) Lay the cigar on a chilled baking sheet in the freezer. Repeat for the remaining cake and filling until there are 18 cigars.

When ready to assemble, unwrap a cigar and randomly place 2 mint leaves around it on one half of the cigar. With a pastry brush, spread some of the remaining melted coating chocolate over the mint leaves. Place 2 more mint leaves on the other half of the cigar, and brush again with chocolate. Return to the freezer and repeat for the remaining cigars. Cover the baking sheet tightly.

To serve, mix the I cup of cocoa powder, $^1/_2$ cup confectioners' sugar, and $^1/_2$ tablespoon cinnamon on a large plate. Take a cigar from the freezer and roll it in the powder mixture. Repeat for the remaining cigars.

Combine the I cup of confectioners' sugar and the $^1/_2$ cup of cocoa powder. Dust individual plates with the mixture. Place the cigars and ice cream on the plates and serve.

YIELD: 18 SERVINGS

Oppostie page: The Smokeless Macanudo

GLOSSARY

Although this glossary is somewhat eclectic, it is heavily based on Spanish words and terms that refer to Latin American ingredients and foods. It includes some definitions that are not used in the book but that will prove helpful to those interested in broadening their knowledge of Nuevo Latino cuisine. Keep in mind that some of the ingredient names will vary from country to country.

Achiote: See annatto.

Adobo: Marinade. Dry adobos are spice rubs for meat, fish, or poultry.

Ancho: Dried form of the poblano chile. Sweet, fruity tones and mild heat.

Angostura bitters: Tart flavoring used mostly for drinks, distilled from plants and herbs. Believed to stimulate the appetite.

Annatto: Also known as achiote. Brick-red seeds of a tree native to the New World, with a mildly acidic, earthy, orange-tinged flavor. Used as a natural coloring to give a yellowish tint to foods, including butter and cheese.

Arroz: Rice.

Bacalao: Dried salt cod, popular throughout Latin America. It should be boiled in several changes of water to remove the salt. Buy the boneless type.

Banana leaves: Traditional wrapping used for steaming foods such as tamals or fish and seafood, especially in tropical regions.

Batido: Tropical chilled milkshake. Made with fruit juices and sweetened milk. Rum may be added for a delicious cocktail.

Bijol: Substitute for the more expensive saffron, used with rice especially. Contains cornflour, cumin, and ground annatto.

Boniato: Tuber also known as white sweet potato, Florida yam, and camote. It looks like a sweet potato on the outside, but is shorter and rounder and has white, sweetish, mealy flesh. The boniato is usually large, averaging $1\frac{1}{2}$ to 2 pounds. Scrub well before using.

Cachucha: Tiny, round chile also known as aji dulce. Usually green, with very little heat but a pungent aroma and an acidic, slightly fruity flavor.

Calabaza: Also called West Indian pumpkin. A large, round, sweet squash, resembling a pumpkin (for which it can be substituted) in its size and orange flesh. Firm texture and sweet flavor.

Causa: Peruvian potato terrine with layers of filling, usually served cold. Some versions are similar to shepherd's pie.

Cava: Spanish sparkling wine.

Ceviche: Name of the dish and technique that originated in Peru; raw fish or seafood is pickled and "cooked" in the acidic juice of citrus fruit (usually lime juice). Ceviches are often flavored with herbs, chiles, and other ingredients.

Chimichurri: Pesto-like condiment from Argentina, traditionally served with churrasco. Made with a base of parsley, garlic, and olive oil.

Chipotle: Smoked jalapeño chile. Available canned, in a sauce ("chipotles en adobo"), and dried.

Chorizo: Spicy Spanish hard pork sausage. Substitute salami. Not to be confused with spicy Mexican chorizo, which is made with fresh pork and is sold in sausage, patty, or bulk form.

Churrasco: Argentinian dish of marinated and grilled skirt steak. The Nicaraguan version is made with filet mignon.

Coco Lopez: Canned sweetened coconut milk.

Coconut milk: Liquid prepared from the meat of fresh coconuts blended with water and strained (or heated and strained). It is most easily available canned.

Conch: Mollusk (pronounced "conk") particularly popular in Florida and the Caribbean. The tough but flavorful meat must first be tenderized before cooking. Mostly available frozen in the United States.

Croqueta: Rolled snack, usually containing a savory filling. Typically croquetas are breaded and fried.

Empanada: Stuffed pastry turnover with savory filling, of Spanish origin. Popular throughout Latin America.

Enchilado: Seafood dish in a spicy tomato-based sauce.

Escabeche: Vinegar-based spicy pickling liquid, marinade, or stew used to preserve cooked vegetables, fish, seafood, or meat.

Frijoles: Beans.

Frita: Cuban burger-style sandwich made with seasoned ground meat and chorizo, topped with thin threads of fried potato.

Fufu: Mashed plantains, flavored with garlic, onion, and bacon.

Guajillo: Dried brownish-red chile with fruity tones.

Guava: Subtropical fruit with green skin and sweet, pink flesh that's popular throughout Latin America. Guava paste is sold in slabs and in canned form; guava marmalade is sold in cans. Puréed guava is available frozen. All forms are available in Latin markets.

Hearts of palm: Also known as *palmitos.* Tender ivory-colored shoots of a type of palm. Mostly available canned, but can be found fresh in Florida.

Huancaina: Peruvian spicy sauce made with cheese and eggs, traditionally served with potatoes.

Malanga: Starchy root vegetable popular throughout Latin America and used much like potato. Nutty, earthy flavor; the yellow to red flesh turns gray when cooked. Also known as yautia and taro.

Manchego: Traditional Spanish sheep milk, semi-firm cheese. Rich and mellow-flavored.

Mandoline: Hand-held slicing machine with adjustable blades. Strongly recommended.

Mariscos: Shellfish.

Mesclun: Mixture of lettuce greens such as Bibb, radicchio, arugula, baby spinach, etc.

Mojo: Spicy (not hot) sauce, particularly popular in Cuba, usually served with cooked foods. Typically, made with garlic, citrus juice, oil, and at least one type of herb.

Muñeta: Puréed black beans.

Ñame: Large tropical tuber with white to yellow flesh. Coarse texture and bland, potato-like flavor. Also known as tropical yam and African yam.

Papa: Potato.

Picadillo: Savory, spicy ground beef, typically cooked with a sofrito, olives, and capers. Often used as a filling or served with rice, black beans, and fried plantains.

Pinton: A semiripe plantain.

Pisco: Peruvian grape liquor similar to the Italian grappa.

Plantain: *Plátano* in Spanish. A member of the banana family that is always used cooked. Sweet, banana-like flavor with a brownish-black skin when ripe; starchy in flavor with yellow skin that's freckled or spotted when semiripe; green skin in unripe state. See page 6 for method to peel the thick skin.

Poblano: Fresh green chile especially popular in Mexico and Central America. In its dried form, it is called the ancho chile.

Pollo: Chicken.

Queso blanco: Salty, firm, white cheese similar to mozzarella or Muenster. Common in Latin American cooking and widely available in Latin markets.

Quinoa: Pronounced "KEEN-wah." A tiny, ancient staple grain cultivated by the Incas that's still grown extensively in the Andean region of South America. High in protein and nutrients, quinoa is becoming increasingly popular in the United States because of its healthful properties. Used like rice or couscous.

Ropa vieja: Beef dish of Spanish origin made with skirt or flank steak in a tomato-based sauce and served with rice. Literally "old clothes" because the meat is shredded and looks like torn-up rags.

Scotch bonnet: Hot chile with fruity tones that's popular in the Caribbean. A close relative of the habanero, which is the hottest chile of all.

Seviche: See ceviche.

Sofrito: Mixture of sautéed vegetables, usually including onion, garlic, bell peppers, tomatoes, herbs, and spices. Sofritos form the foundation of many stews and meat dishes.

Star anise: Type of anise native to China and one of the Chinese "five spices." The dried fruit has a licorice-like flavor.

Tamal: Corn-based appetizer or snack, sometimes served plain but typically containing a savory filling. Tamals are usually wrapped in a dried corn husk and steamed, but fresh husks and banana leaves are also used as wrappings.

Tamarind: Popular Latin American legume, related to beans. Pods yield a pulp with a sweet and sour flavor. Tamarind is widely used in Latin America as a flavoring. Blocks of tamarind pulp or paste as well as tamarind juice, which comes in fresh or frozen form, are available at Latin and Asian markets.

Tasajo: Traditional dried salt-cured beef (*carne seca*), rather like jerky (although it cannot be eaten plain as is jerky). Available in Latin markets; corned beef can be substituted in recipes.

Tostones: Refried flattened plantains.

Turmeric: Spice native to Asia, used mainly as a food coloring (for example, in American-style prepared mustard).

Vigoron: Nicaraguan salad made with shredded cabbage.

Yuca: Root vegetable native to Africa, also known as cassava or manioc. Yuca (pronounced "YOO-ka") is not to be confused with yucca (pronounced "YUCK-a"), which is a genus of plants in the *Agave* family with sword-shaped leaves and white blooms. Yuca is a tuber and grows underground, like potatoes. Commonly used throughout Latin America and the Caribbean. Elongated shape with a brown skin, a starchy white flesh, and a bland, slightly sweet potato-like flavor.

SOURCES

The majority of ingredients in this book are available at your local Latin market. While traveling in this country, I have also found some Latin fruits and vegetables in the major chain supermarkets from time to time. If, however, you cannot locate what you need, you might want to contact a manager at one of the following markets:

El Camaguey Meat Market
(carries Latin ingredients in addition to meats)
10925 Venice Blvd., West Los Angeles, CA 90034
310-839-4037

La Palma
2884 24th St., San Francisco, CA 94110
415-647-1500

FOR HIGH-QUALITY EGGS
The Country Hen
P.O. Box 333, Hubbardston, MA 01452
978-928-5333, 978-928-5414 (fax)

A dependable source for certified salmonella-free eggs. Offers mail-order service.

INDEX